I Forgive You

Previous publications by Judith A. Doctor:

Christian Dreamwork: 33 Ways To Discover Divine Treasure In Dreams

Dream Treasure: Learning the Language of Heaven

I Forgive You

How Heart-Based Forgiveness Sets You Free

Judith A. Doctor

Doctor Resources

I Forgive You: How Heart-Based Forgiveness Sets You Free

Published in the United States by
Doctor Resources
www.judithdoctor.com

ISBN: 978-0-9837917-4-4

Doctor Resources provides educational and inspirational publications and other resources that nurture Christian spiritual maturity and transformative growth through the Holy Spirit.

Cover photo by Penywise at Morguefile.com

Editor, Designer, Producer: Gerald R. Doctor
geraldrdoctor@gmail.com

Contents

Preface

Lack of forgiveness is killing us. Everywhere we look we see anger, hatred, violence, and murder on the streets of America. Even in the church.

Families are riddled with unforgiveness, causing breaks in relationships and unhappiness with others and within ourselves. Damaging effects of unforgiveness impact our lives on every level, especially our emotional and psychological well-being.

In the Gospels, Jesus tried to make us aware of the dangers of unforgiveness. He said if we don't forgive others from our heart, we will open ourselves to torturers—the kingdom of darkness.

Even with this warning, we seldom wonder whether any of our problems—emotional and mental ills, family brokenness, physical symptoms—might be linked to unforgiveness. We are ignorant of the price we will pay … *if we let the sun go down on our anger.*

Most people do not know there is a relationship between forgiving others and our psychological, physical, spiritual, and social well-being. Forgiving others produces a more positive attitude, makes our bodies healthier, and gives us a higher quality of life. Hanging onto painful memories and past wounds can make us more susceptible to illnesses.

Professionals use forgiveness to treat all types of troubles: anxiety and depression, compulsions, marriage and family relationships, family-of-origin issues, abuse, trauma, divorce, bereavement, and other losses.

Numerous studies prove the healing power of forgiveness. In some areas forgiveness therapy is even integrated into the protocols for treating cancer. If helping professionals use forgiveness as a powerful healing tool, how can we in the church do any less?

When we pray the Lord's Prayer, we ask God to forgive us our debts in the same way that we forgive our debtors. Yet countless church-goers lug around a load of guilt and grudges. I have listened to them recite their list of wrongs against someone and then say, "But I have forgiven them." Many do not even recognize that they are holding deep-seated resentments from long ago—even from childhood.

For most Christians, Jesus' assertion that "He who the Son sets free, is free indeed" is mere theological knowledge, not a reality they have known, felt, and proved by experience.

If you listen inside our homes and churches, you'll hear reproachful voices and be privy to a list of grievances. Look into their eyes—which reflect the heart—and you'll see the lack of joy and peace in their faces. They are plagued by critical hearts, shallow relationships, and a lack of genuine compassion and love for people around them.

Is it because we don't understand what forgiveness *is* and *is not*? Or the biblical basis of forgiving from the heart? Or is it because we want to take revenge, invoking the "eye-for-an-eye" method?

Perhaps the worst reason is rejecting the blood of Jesus Christ as not enough payment for someone's sin against us. Throughout history in every culture and society, blood is required to resolve the debts of offences committed against others. More than 2000 years ago, God provided us with the sacrificial blood of Christ so debts can be forgiven.

Failure to forgive—or to receive forgiveness—is a crucial barrier to experiencing the peace, joy, and freedom that Jesus Christ made possible. The kind of forgiveness that Jesus asks of his followers is this: forgiveness must take place in our heart, not only in our mind.

The idea for this book was spawned by a German veterinarian attending one of our retreats in Austria. After I spoke on biblical forgiveness, he excitedly said, "Now I understand what's wrong with people. Their hearts are so hard. We don't understand forgiveness, and we don't do what Jesus said, 'forgive from the heart.'"

In my inner healing ministry and counseling practice I have often witnessed the damage of unforgiveness in people's lives. Heart-based forgiveness means you allow your emotional core to be touched, release your right for revenge, and let go of the record of wrongs you've been collecting.

In this book, I focus on helping you learn how to forgive others *and* yourself. I describe clearly the process of forgiving, outlining 12 steps that will set you free from the heavy load of resentment, anger, and hatred.

A quick look through the chapters

In one sense this is a Bible study book because I base everything on Scripture. The first words in the first chapter are those of Jesus Christ instructing us to forgive anyone we have something against—so our Heavenly Father will forgive us.

Chapter 1 introduces this marvelous tool God has given us. Forgiving from your heart has tremendous power to heal your life and set you free.

Unforgiveness can be an immense problem. In Chapter 2 you will discover the link between resentment and many health problems.

The potential for unforgiveness to spiral completely out of control is covered in Chapter 3. Refusal to forgive opens the door to demonic-fueled pressures that can lead downward from revenge to hatred to violence.

In Chapter 4 we talk about Divine Laws that govern the universe, including the need to restore balance when an offense is perpetrated against someone.

The necessity for blood to achieve forgiveness is developed in Chapter 5. The blood of Jesus empowers you to forgive even your most odious offenders. Providing an understanding of this concept is one of the most important contributions of this book.

The detailed discussion in Chapter 6 about what biblical forgiveness really means will help you grasp all that's involved in saying those three simple—but profound—words, "I forgive you."

Many Christian people greatly misunderstand what forgiveness really is and what it is not. Chapter 7 will help straighten out a lot of that for you. Expect some surprises.

Chapter 8 describes the pathway to letting go of an offense at a deep heart level. I break it down into steps, so you can acknowledge your wounding, take account of what happened, and release someone from the debt they owe you.

Chapter 9 is a brief Bible study on three concepts that are central to forgiveness: sin, repentance, and faith. Whether you skipped catechism or need a refresher, these bedrock truths of Christianity need to be understood at a deeper level.

Often people have trouble coming to grips with forgiveness. Chapter 10 discusses various reasons why we refuse to forgive. Perhaps here you'll discover your particular hang-up and finally be able to say those words that set you free.

God has given us a choice of life or death, blessing or curse. In Chapter 11 we see that forgiveness is an area loaded with biblical blessings to enjoy.

Finally, in Chapter 12, I lead you through the process of actually forgiving your offenders. You'll be doing business with God as you make peace in your heart with everyone who has ever hurt you. Be sure to include yourself!

This book on heart-based forgiveness will change your life.

You'll experience newfound freedom in your relationships. Release from painful memories. A lighter load on your immune system. Free from guilt. Free to love. Free to move your life forward.

1

When You Stand Praying, Forgive

> *Whenever you stand praying, forgive, if you have anything against anyone; so that your Father also who is in heaven may forgive you your transgressions" (Mark 11:26).*

Jesus Christ instructs his followers throughout the Gospels to forgive others—even their enemies—whenever they stand praying.

> *Pray, then, in this way: "Our Father who art in heaven, Hallowed by Thy name. Thy kingdom come. Thy will be done, on earth as it is in heaven ... And forgive us our debts, as we also have forgiven our debtors" ... For if you forgive men their transgressions, your heavenly Father will also forgive you. But if you do not forgive men, then your Father will not forgive your transgressions (Matt 6:9-10, 14-15).*

On Sundays we pray, "Forgive us our debts as we have forgiven our debtors." Yet many of us do not do what He says. Why? Why do we not forgive?

Everywhere we see Christians held in bondage by deeply-held resentment, anger, and hatred. Living in an age of retribution, they are holding grudges and grievances, and a desire to punish the people who have hurt them.

As we counsel them, we hear echoes of buried resentments and anger from long ago. At the time their anger may have been righteously appropriate, but, because they failed to forgive, their anger turned inward and became deep-seated. Their personality became poisoned by the entangled roots of bitterness embedded in their hearts.

When they speak, their words are sharp and biting, inflicting pain on the people around them. Over time, the channels of their hearts have become clogged and they are unable to function freely with the people they care about: their conversations are stifled and stilted, their affections restrained.

Unforgiveness closes the heart

Unforgiveness causes our hearts to harden, making it difficult to love others. St. Paul tells us to "walk no longer as the Gentiles walk … excluded from the life of God … because of the *hardness of their heart*" (Eph 4:17-18).

When we are hurt, our hearts naturally want to close up. When this happens, we begin to emotionally shut down, close off, and isolate ourselves from others. We may withdraw our gifts and talents from our Christian communities. God's love and life are unable to flow through us anymore.

As a result, we do not use what the Lord has given us and we lose what we have. We dry up inside. Our hearts grow cold.

People coming for help complain of feeling stuck, powerless, and lonely—unable to move forward in their lives. Their hardened, stony hearts cannot experience the presence of Christ or love the people around them.

Healing Power of Forgiveness

In recent years, research has proven the healing power of forgiveness. Studies found that forgiveness can help lead people to emotional and physical healing.[1] People who forgive experience a noticeable decrease in anxiety, depression, hopelessness, inner emptiness, and an increase in self-esteem. They are more satisfied with their lives than the people who do not forgive.[2]

Offers release from destructive emotions

Social scientists discovered that forgiveness is a key to healing psychological wounds. One clinical psychologist wrote, "Forgiveness offers a pathway out of the kind of emotional and psychological pain that repeats and repeats itself throughout our life."[3]

Sociologist Hobart Mowrer found that guilt was more detrimental to our emotional and mental health than childhood deprivation or neglect.[4] Guilt damages our capacity to love others and to love ourselves. It manipulates us, influencing our choices and the motivations in our heart. It closes us off from intimate relationships with the people around us.

Forgiveness is the most significant factor in both spiritual and psychological healing, a crucial stage in the healing of our soul and spirit. It offers us release from the debilitating effects of guilt, shame, anger, resentment, and rage.

Restorative power of forgiveness

Today forgiveness is considered to offer a highly significant and promising mode of healing in the counseling room. It is being used for all manner of problems: anger and depression, catharsis and peace with cancer patients, family-of-origin issues, sexual abuse and compulsions.[5]

Research provides clear evidence that forgiveness is a powerful tool to help us recover from abuse, bereavement, trauma, addiction, abortion, divorce, and other losses. It enables us to tap into powerful spiritual resources that foster our healing.

Forgiveness is also being used to identify and resolve conflicted family relationships.[6] It helps adolescents who felt unloved by their parents. Importantly, forgiveness has been identified as one of the top ten characteristics in a long-term first marriage.[7]

> **Forgiveness is a force that heals and builds, while non-forgiveness divides and destroys. To forgive means peace and freedom in an individual's heart, and love and openness in our relationships. Non-forgiveness kills the spirit of love within us and between us. It holds on to anger and resentment, and thereby to coldness and pain. Forgiveness fosters our growth; non-forgiveness shuts us down—Harry Aponte.[8]**

Christian psychologist, Dr. Charles Zeiders describes the restorative impact of forgiveness as a "psychological healing complemented by lightness of spirit." He says, "Because forgiveness so powerfully lifts souls to the experience of new psychological life, I call this effect *The Resurrection Effect.*" He explains that "forgiveness has the power to bring about individual and interpersonal healing through removing emotional burdens, bringing peace, and in some cases restoring relationships."[9]

Forgiveness—The Greatest Tool of Power

More than 2000 years ago, God provided us with the greatest tool of power ever given to humanity: forgiveness.[10] Because of the work of Jesus Christ on the cross, we can be forgiven for our sins and transgressions. Because his sacrificial blood was given in payment for all of humanity's transgressions, we can forgive the people who sin against us—empowering us to keep our hearts open to God and the people around us.

"Momma, I'm so sorry"

Here is how I found freedom from guilt and healing for a wound in my heart:

A motherly woman was praying with me for inner healing. Suddenly she stopped and said, "Judy, there is a fear in you which is connected to the death of an animal." Immediately, my mind snapped back to something that happened many years ago. I'd been only five.

It was a warm summer day and my cousin stopped by and invited me to walk with her to the drugstore. I ran inside to ask my Mom: "Yes, you can go," she said, "but make sure the gate is shut so Nellie [the dog] can't get out and follow you."

Several blocks from home, I heard a dog bark and turned around: there was Nellie chasing after us with her tail wagging. "Go back! Go back!" I yelled, but I didn't take her back. A few blocks later, I heard a thud. I turned around and saw Nellie writhing in the street. She'd been hit by a car.

As I told my friend about this, I could see my mother weeping over the death of her dog. From deep within, I felt pain, like it was a bubble, moving up toward the surface and I cried out "Momma! Momma, I always disobeyed you. I'm so sorry. Please forgive me!"

My friend wrapped her loving arms around me and held me as I cried out my pain to the Lord, confessed my guilt, and received his forgiveness. And the wound in my heart was healed; no more guilt resided there!

Importance of the heart

Physically the heart is our most vital central organ. Symbolically, the heart refers to the core and center of everything, the source of the hidden springs of our personal life. Everything we do flows out from the heart.

Understanding the importance of his heart to God, King David says:

> *How blessed is the man ... in whose heart are the highways to Zion (Ps 84:5).*

> *Search me O God, and know my heart; try me and know my anxious thoughts; and see if there be any way of pain in me (Ps 139:23-24).*

God offers us the promise of a new heart, a heart sensitive to the needs of others. Jesus cares how we relate to the people around us. This is why He is concerned with forgiveness and why we must forgive from our heart.

> *Create in me a clean heart O God (Ps 51:10).*

Forgiveness opens the heart

St. Paul also recognized the problem of the heart in the church at Corinth. Even though he and Timothy had been hurt (imprisoned, dishonored, regarded as deceivers), he wrote:

> *Our mouth has spoken freely to you, O Corinthians, our heart is opened wide. (2 Cor 6:11).*

Forgiveness enables us to keep our hearts open and flowing with warmth and affection to the people we care about. Our affections will not be restrained, our mouths will speak freely, our discourse will not be stifled or stilted.

The Lord said to our friend whose son was into drugs, "Keep your heart open to your son." In other words, don't become angry and shut him out of your lives.

Forgiveness offers us the key that opens the door to God's peace, joy, and love in our hearts.

> *If we love one another, God abides in us, and His love is perfected in us (1 John 4:12).*

The heart must be postured with a "will to forgive."[11] Conversion of the heart is the critical stage toward forgiveness.

We must watch over our heart and recognize when it closes toward someone we are in relationship with. Here are some tips:

- Pay attention to how you feel toward the person, asking if your affections are restrained, bound.
- Notice how you talk with the person. Does your conversation feel natural and free-flowing or constricted?
- Notice whether or not you are avoiding the person.
- Are you maintaining a list of wrongs the person has done?
- Pray and ask the Lord to open your heart in his way and his time.

As you consider forgiveness, it is vital to seek the Holy Spirit's help. The Holy Spirit will bring to your attention who you need to forgive and will empower you to do the impossible, to forgive from your heart.

Reflection

1. Why is forgiving others important to Jesus?
2. How does unforgiveness affect the heart?
3. What makes forgiveness so powerful?

I Forgive You

2

High Cost of Unforgiveness

So shall My heavenly Father also do to you, if each of you does not forgive his brother from your heart (Matt 18:35)

Are you aware that we can experience failures simply because of ignorance? The prophet Isaiah writes, "My people go into exile (captivity) for their lack of knowledge" (Isa 5:13). The prophet Hosea states, "My people are destroyed for lack of knowledge" (Hosea 4:6). And in the New Testament, the apostle Paul often questions the early believers, "Do you not know … ?"

Many Christians are ignorant of the high cost of unforgiveness. They do not understand how or why unforgiveness affects their lives. In the Gospels, Jesus Christ links forgiving others to answered prayers and well-being.

He also warns that if we do not forgive from the heart, we will be turned over to the torturers. In his epistles, St. Paul tells the early believers that unforgiveness will open the door to Satan and his schemes.

Unforgiveness Opens Us to Torture

In response to Peter's question about how many times he must forgive, Jesus tells a story about the revengeful servant who, although he had been forgiven his debt, had his fellow man, who owed him money, thrown into prison.

When the servant falls on his knees before his master, the master feels compassion for the man, because he knows that the man does not have the means to repay him, and releases (forgives) him from the debt.

But then, the forgiven man finds his fellow servant who owes him a small sum of money and tries to force him to pay it back. He even places his hand around the guy's neck, trying to choke it out of him. Failing that, he has his friend thrown into prison.

When hearing of his behavior, the master calls him and says,

> *"You wicked slave; I forgave you all that debt because you entreated me. Should you not also have had mercy on your fellow slave, even as I had mercy on you?"*
>
> *And his lord, moved with anger, handed him over to the torturers until he should repay all that was owed him (Matt 18:32-33)*
>
> *Jesus turns to his followers and says,*
>
> *"My heavenly Father will also do the same to you, if each of you does not forgive his brother from your heart" (Matt 18:35).*

In this parable, Jesus establishes the reality that unforgiveness carries a high price tag: *torture!* Modern research scientists have discovered the same truth. Resentment, anger, and rage affect our health, our mind and emotions, our social relationships, and our walk with God.

Makes us physically sick

It is well-established that most physical sicknesses have an emotional component. Over two-thirds of hospital beds are occupied by patients who are put there because of their inability to organize and discipline their emotions. It has been estimated that fifty to seventy-five percent of patients are sick because of the influence of thought patterns and emotions upon their physical bodies.[12]

Negative emotions like anger and resentment take a great toll on our bodies. Studies have demonstrated a strong relationship between hostility and heart disease as well as with other diseases like ulcers, gastritis, cancer, and colitis. They also show that chronically angry people die earlier than non-hostile people.[13]

Studies have verified the positive power of forgiveness on our well-being. For instance, people who forgive are more likely to enjoy lower blood pressure, a stronger immune system, and a drop in the stress hormones circulating in their blood. Their back pain, stomach problems, and headaches may disappear. They report reduced anger, anxiety, depression, and PTSD symptoms; higher self-esteem; and more hopefulness about their future.

> **What I have come to see ... is how intimately the forgiveness of sins is connected with bodily and emotional healing. They are not separate. In fact, far from being a sign of God's blessing, much physical sickness is a direct sign that we are not right with God or our neighbor – Francis MacNutt.[14]**

Refusing to forgive may not directly cause disease, but the negative effects of holding on to hurtful memories and past injuries can weaken your immune system. You become more susceptible to illnesses and diseases, including cancer, so says webMD.com, the respected medical advice web site.

Dr. Steven Standiford, chief of surgery at Cancer Treatment Centers of America, claims: "It's important to treat emotional wounds or disorders because they really can hinder someone's reactions to the treatments — even someone's willingness to pursue treatment." In fact, forgiveness therapy is now an integral part of cancer treatment at the center.

Closes off intimate relationships

Chronic anger has been proven to damage interpersonal relationships, causing loneliness and loss of social support.[15] Reportedly, unresolved anger is a key issue in failing marriages. Couples with high levels of hostility have more destructive communications. People who cannot resolve their anger tend to turn away from intimate relationships and lose passion.

Forgiveness reduces our anger and resentment and often leads to an improvement in personal relationships with our family, friends and community.

Blocks our physical and emotional healing

When Jesus healed the man at the pool of Bethsaida, He made a direct relationship between sin and sickness. He told the man to not sin anymore (John 5:1-9). Some authors suggest that unforgiveness may be an important block to receiving healing in our bodies and souls.[16]

Dr. Zeiders describes how unforgiveness acts as a barrier to healing deep psychological wounds in his article, "*A Christian Depth Psychology of Forgiveness Leading to the Resurrection Effect.*"

In his book, *Healing*, former Catholic priest Francis MacNutt wrote, "I have found that many sins do not block God's healing power to the same extent as does a lack of forgiveness. I understand better than I used to why Jesus laid such a heavy stress on forgiving enemies when he talked about prayer … He often seems to connect forgiving enemies with the Father's answering prayers."[17]

Imprisons our wounds

When someone sins against us unjustly, we sustain a wound in our heart. We respond to the painful wound by becoming angry and resentful. To balance the scales of justice, someone must pay for the pain we experienced: either the person who hurt us or even our self.

Consciously or unconsciously, we desire to hurt someone. Consequently our resentment and revenge become deeply entrenched in the wound, causing it to feel even more painful.

> *My heart is wounded (smitten like grass and withered away) within me (Ps 102:4).*
>
> *People weighed down with iniquity ... From the sole of the foot even unto the head there is no soundness in it, but wounds, and bruises, and putrefying sores; they have not been closed, neither bound up, neither mollified with ointment (Isa 1:4-6).*
>
> *Thus says the Lord, 'Your wound is incurable, and your injury is serious, there is no one to plead your cause; no healing for your sore, no recovery for you' (Jer 30:12).*

Our wounds, now imprisoned, are cut off from the healing presence and love of Jesus Christ. The only way out is to turn to God for healing, repent of the desire to take revenge, and forgive those who wounded or hurt us. The act of repentance enables us to humble ourselves, placing ourselves before God in a receiving position.

Causes personality imbalance and disintegration

Many emotions can paralyze and debilitate us because they produce an unhealthy spiritual and mental condition. Fear and anxiety are disintegrating enemies of human personality. They clog up normal sources of emotional, spiritual, and intellectual power.

We become bogged down by resentment, fear, and guilt; our emotional ills turn in upon ourselves and sap our energy, reducing efficiency. Unable to expel our anxieties which have turned inward on our personality, we enter into a state of dis-ease and fall prey to many forms of ill health.

When negative emotions such as grudges, ill-will, anger, and irritation accumulate to a certain weight, the personality can't support them and gives way. We say, "I'm going to pieces, falling apart, or flying to pieces," which describes a threatened state of imbalance and disintegration.[18] The roar of these negative emotions also overpowers the gentle voice of the Spirit and chokes off the stream of God's life flowing through us.

Unforgiveness Opens the Door to Satan

In his letter to the Christians at Ephesus, Paul warns the early believers of the dangers of unforgiveness. He says it will open the doorway to the kingdom of Satan and allow all manner of evil things to trouble us.

> *Be angry, and yet do not sin; do not let the sun go down on your anger, and do not give the devil an opportunity [a place] (Eph 4:26, 27).*
>
> *For where jealousy and selfish ambition exist, there is disorder and every evil thing (Jas 3:16).*
>
> *For indeed what I have forgiven ... I did it for your sakes in the presence of Christ, in order that no advantage be taken of us by Satan; for we are not ignorant of his schemes (2 Cor 2:10-11).*

Allows Satan legal access to us

When we refuse to forgive someone, destructive spiritual powers and rulers of the darkness have the "legal right" to access us.

When we will not let go of the sins of others, we are keeping that person under the "bondage of our judgment." Demonic bondages often stem from broken relationships of trust between people.[19] When we hold another's sins and do not forgive them, we are holding a curse upon ourselves.

> *If you forgive the sins of any, their sins have been forgiven them; if you retain the sins of any, they have been retained (John 20:23).*
>
> *I say to you that everyone who is angry with his brother shall be guilty before the court; and whoever shall say to his brother, "Raca" [empty headed, good for nothing], shall be guilty before the supreme court; and whoever shall say, "You fool," shall be guilty enough to go into the fiery hell (Matt 5:22).*

Once unforgiveness gains a foothold, we develop more serious spiritual problems. Evils like resentment, revenge, rage, hatred, violence, and murder begin to consume our hearts and minds, forming destructive strongholds within the structures of our personality. Note, these are spiritual problems—not just psychological symptoms!

Hinders God's protecting grace

Unforgiveness, resentment, and anger open us to demonic bondage and the devil's power. Failure to forgive moves us out from God's protecting grace.

In the story of Cain and Abel, the Lord was pleased with Abel's offering of a sacrificial lamb, whereas, He rejected Cain's offering of fruit from his garden. Why? Cain had not followed the Lord's instruction about how to resolve sin—a sacrificial lamb.

When Cain became *very angry* by the favor shown to his brother, the Lord warned:

> *If you do well, will not your countenance be lifted up? And if you do not do well, sin is crouching at the door; and its desire is for you, but you must master it (see Genesis 4:1-16).*

Cain failed to receive forgiveness from God for his sinful rebellion or forgive his brother for doing it right. His unresolved sin brought God's judgment down on him. He was condemned to roam the earth as a vagrant, unable to bring forth fruit from it. He lived in exile outside the presence of his Creator. We must recognize that *we cannot do whatever we want*—without consequence.

Our enemy wants to destroy us

Jesus did three things while on earth: He healed the sick and oppressed, treating sickness as an enemy. He taught that the kingdom of God is available to us here on earth. And He dealt with demonic activity, setting people free from evil spirits.

> *God anointed Jesus of Nazareth with the Holy Spirit and power, and He went around doing good and healing all who were under the power of the devil (Acts 10:38).*

> *They brought to him many who were possessed with demons; and He cast out the spirits with a word, and healed all who were sick (Matt 8:16).*

> *The news about Him spread throughout all Syria; and they brought to Him all who were ill, those suffering with various diseases and pains, demoniacs, epileptics, paralytics; and He healed them (Matt 4:24).*

From the work of Jesus, it is clear that the kingdom of darkness and demonic beings are involved with physical, mental, and emotional problems. Jesus treated sickness as a work of an enemy. We need to recognize that we have an enemy who wants to kill, rob, and destroy us.

> *Be sober, be watchful, because your adversary, the devil, walks around like a roaring lion, seeking someone to devour (1 Pet 5:8).*

Unforgiveness Grieves the Holy Spirit

Not only does unforgiveness open us to the domain of darkness but according to St. Paul it also grieves the Holy Spirit:

> *Do not grieve the Holy Spirit of God ... be kind to one another, tender-hearted, forgiving each other, just as God in Christ has forgiven you (Eph 4:30-32).*

> *You men who are stiff-necked and uncircumcised in heart and ears are always resisting the Holy Spirit; you are doing just as your fathers did (Acts 7:51).*

The Holy Spirit was sent to dwell within each believer because He has a work to do in bringing us to salvation and wholeness. The work of the Holy Spirit is to teach us, guide us, fill us with God's power and authority, and give us spiritual gifts.

> *The Helper, the Holy Spirit, whom the Father will send in My name, He will teach you all things (John 14:26).*

> *When the Spirit of truth comes, He will guide you into all the truth (John 16:13).*

> *Now we have received, not the spirit of the world, but the Spirit who is from God, that we might know the things freely given to us by God (1 Cor. 2:9-12).*

The Holy Spirit reveals Jesus Christ in us and guides us into the truth. In the journey to spiritual growth and wholeness, the power of the Holy Spirit working within us is essential. If we grieve the Holy Spirit by refusing to forgive others, we are robbing ourselves of the help we need.

Reflection

1. What do the words of Jesus about being turned over to "torturers" mean to you?
2. Identify ways that unforgiveness can affect us.
3. Why does unforgiveness open the door to demonic spirits?

3

Downward Spiral of Unforgiveness

Be angry, and yet do not sin; do not let the sun go down on your anger, and do not give the devil an opportunity [a place] (Eph 4:26, 27).

We need to understand the pernicious nature of unforgiveness. It is a luxury that we dare not indulge in, because it leads us down the road to far greater evils. Following is a description of the downward spiral unforgiveness will take you on.

1. Create a record of wrongs

Unforgiveness starts with the feeling that we have been injured or wronged by someone or something. If we do not forgive from the heart, we will create a record of their wrongs against us and begin to repeat them over and over.

A dream in the night

Here is my experience with reciting my mother's wrongs.

A few years ago, I suddenly became aware that I needed to forgive my mother for failing to call me by my name. For most of her life she couldn't seem to call me "Judith;" instead she'd call me by my sister's name. This bothered me, even though most mothers, including me, often mix up their children's names.

On her death bed, when I said, "I love you, Mom," she couldn't say, "I love you" back." But she said, "I love *all* of you children." I'd held these offenses against her for many years, often reciting them to others. Then one day the Lord opened my eyes, and I forgave her.

That very night I dreamed she'd just died. I could see her lying dead in her bed. My sister and I were busy cleaning up her things, when suddenly my mother opened her eyes and looked right at me. Her eyes filled with great love for me. Then she closed her eyes and was again gone. I awoke feeling great joy; I knew I was forgiven.

2. Resentment grows, beginning a feud

As we rehash someone's wrongs, our feelings of resentment toward them grow. The offense creates a barrier between us and a break occurs in our relationship. Our heart closes to the person who hurt us. Consciously or unconsciously, a feud has broken out.

Resentment is the feeling of displeasure and indignation caused by the sense of being injured or offended.

You can recognize resentment by the negative feelings of displeasure or indignation and the continual replaying in your mind of their wrongs committed against you. I have listened to clients say, "There has not been a day in my life when I have not remembered what he or she did to me."

Creates feedback loop

For you who want to understand how this works, here is an explanation. Note that there are two things going on: the presence of painful arousal and your trigger thoughts.

Anger begins when we experience either physical or emotional pain. This pain produces a strong arousal within us so that we need to get rid of it (discharge it) and reduce our stress. So what do we do? We make someone responsible for our pain and we begin to blame, criticize, or judge them.

> **The arousal of pain leads to blaming trigger thoughts, which lead to anger and more trigger thoughts and more anger in an escalating downward spiral. Thoughts and angry feelings become a feedback loop that can be self-perpetuating.**
>
> **It is often the feedback loop that keeps anger simmering for hours or even days without letup. It isn't possible to get angry without the presence of both painful arousal and trigger thoughts—McKay & Paleg.[20]**

3. Leads to a desire to retaliate, take revenge

Resentment leads to a desire to take vengeance, to retaliate. We look for ways to get back at the person who hurt us. We want them to hurt in the same way they hurt us. Dr. Zeiders refers to this as a *Will to Punish.*

By making someone pay for what they did to us, we think we can get rid of the pain we feel and make our wounds heal. But the Bible tells us not to do this:

> *Never take your own revenge, beloved, but leave room for the wrath of God, for it is written, 'Vengeance is Mine, I will repay,' says the Lord (Rom 12:19).*

When we find ourselves believing we are justified in making others pay for their wrongs against us, we need to take care. We are not God, and we have no right to judge others!

4. Anger increases, leading to rage and hostility

Trying to punish others will create even more anger, causing us to feel irritable and easily provoked. We are quick to lash out with our tongue or to cut others off. Negative thoughts consume our mind and we use behaviors like stonewalling, procrastination, criticism, whining, sulking, or grumpiness to show our anger.

Let everyone be quick to hear, slow to speak and slow to anger; for the anger of man does not achieve the righteousness of God (Jas 1:19-20).

I say to you that everyone who is angry with his brother shall be guilty before the court; and whoever shall say to his brother, "Raca" [empty headed, good for nothing], shall be guilty before the supreme court; and whoever shall say, "You fool," shall be guilty enough to go into the fiery hell (Matt 5:21).

Therapists acknowledge that ventilating anger doesn't help; it only increases or even prolongs it, making it easier for us to get angry again in the future.[21] Experts also suggest that people who experience their anger as rewarding and useful are less willing to let it go.

Drs. Allender & Longman suggest that anger vocalizes a core question we have about God: Is God just or will He let the wicked win and prevail against me? They say, "Unrighteous anger dulls the pain of desperation and aggressively demands justice; since God fails to protect us, we are justified in taking matters into our own hands. Anger attempts to rectify God's passivity by empowering us to act instead of waiting vulnerably for God to do something."[22]

5. Hatred flourishes

As anger increases, hatred moves into our heart. Hatred says the person who hurt us does not have the right to exist anymore, especially in our presence. We find it difficult to stay in the same room with the person. We wish we could eliminate them from our lives.

If someone says, 'I love God,' and hates his brother, he is a liar; for the one who does not love his brother whom he has seen, cannot love God whom he has not seen (1 John 4:19-21).

For some people their hatred turns inward against themselves. They hate themselves rather than the person who hurt them—perhaps from fear they will lose their love. The self-hatred becomes embedded in their psychological core, buried deep in their subconscious: they live with the feeling they have no right to exist and no identity.

Freed from self-hatred

Here's my experience with self-hatred. Since I didn't want to hate my Mom or Grandmother, it was easier to turn my hatred against myself.

For six months I prayed, "Lord, there is a lie somewhere in the depths of my personality; would you heal it?" Then I dreamed of a tiny sore on my thigh opened up right down to the bone. I awoke with the sense that God was going to heal something.

Two days later, my husband and I were discussing the idea that our earliest memory often contains our view of the world and our place in it. I shared my earliest memory with him:

I'm 2 ½ years old, looking at my mother holding my new baby brother through a window. When I start crying for my mother, my grandmother becomes angry with me and mocks me, thus wounding my soul.

As I told Gerald this painful experience, I began to cry—it sounded like a broken-hearted child. In the next hour, I saw two negative beliefs woven into the structure of my personality as a result of this traumatic experience: I wasn't loved, and I wasn't important to my Mom. These lies had been woven into the fabric of my personality.

As I saw these destructive beliefs, the Lord showed me that they were not true, just lies. My mother had loved me and I was important to her. Then I saw that as a result of these lies, I had rejected myself and entered into self-hatred. This self-rejection and self-hatred was embedded in a core wound buried in my subconscious.

eople who are supposed to love me don't, then .iate me."

6. Violence starts

Studies show that chronic anger leads to verbal and physical assault.[23] When hatred turns to violence, we may act like a spoiled child having a temper tantrum—throwing things or using our hands to hit, slap, or push others.

Note that anger is different from aggression: anger is an *emotion*, whereas aggression is a *behavior*, something you do with verbal or physical assault.[24]

Through our behaviors, we're saying, "I want to wipe you off the face of the earth, but before I do this, you are going to experience my pain. You are going to know what you have done to me." If our hatred turns inward, we try to hurt our self, perhaps using destructive self-talk, not caring for our self, or being accident prone.

May evil hunt the violent man speedily (Ps 140:11).

The Lord tests the righteous ... the one who loves violence His soul hates (Ps 11:5).

7. Murderous actions begin

When violence turns to murder, we want to physically wipe the offender off the face of the earth. However, most of us do not use a knife or gun, but we try to destroy someone using our words. We verbally abuse them or assassinate their character. People who hate themselves may turn to addictions or even try to take their own lives.

Jesus said, 'You shall not commit murder' (Matt 19:18).

Everyone who hates his brother is a murderer; and you know that no murderer has eternal life abiding in him (1 John 3:15).

Tip: Try going to God and showing Him the pain you *feel* when someone hurts you. Ask for his grace to come, and then wait for it!

Reflection

1. How do you handle your resentment? Your anger?
2. How does hatred manifest itself?
3. Listen to the people around you (or yourself) and see if you can recognize a "record of wrongs."

I Forgive You

4

Balancing the Scales of Justice

A man injures his neighbor ... so shall it be done to him: fracture for fracture, eye for eye, tooth for tooth (Lev 24:19-20).

The desire to punish people who unjustly hurt or offend us seems very natural and reasonable to us. Indeed, it is part of our very nature to demand retribution for the wrongs we suffer: "You hurt me; I must hurt you back."

The Bible refers to this as "an eye for an eye" or "a tooth for a tooth" method (also see Ex 21:24; Matt 5:38-44). This natural response is inherent in the legality of God's created universe.

Legality of the universe

God has bound Himself to keep his principles of divine jurisprudence. He is a just God. The legality of his universe demands nothing less than justice. Agnes Sanford said, "God does nothing except by law. But He has provided enough power within his laws to do anything that is in accordance with his will."[25]

God simply will not violate his legal principles, because they are "part of his creation and a direct expression of his divine nature."[26] This is what makes God so trustworthy. He cannot be manipulated or coerced, like parents are. His hand moves in direct relationship to his divine laws: He works in accordance with his established laws.

Everything governed by the same principle

An underlying principle of God's created order says that "all things must come into balance or equilibrium." The legality of the universe requires that *all things come to resolution, balance, i.e., justified.* This holds true for natural laws, moral laws, and spiritual laws. God has not made one law for the natural and another for the spiritual.[27]

We see this principle operating in physics and chemistry. The law of physics says for every action there must be an equal and opposite reaction. Every chemistry equation or formula must balance. All these laws are intended to restore balance in the universe.

God's Moral and Spiritual Laws

God's moral and spiritual laws are alive and active in the universe—*even* if we are ignorant of them. We cannot escape them. However, if honored, consciously or unconsciously, they will work to maintain harmony in our lives, restore health and wholeness in us, and release God's blessings to us.

(The following ideas are adapted from John & Paula Sandford.[28])

The law of justice

The law of justice says that *all wrongs must be resolved.* When someone is wronged by someone else, an account is opened, a debt created. The law of justice requires the person who committed the wrong be held accountable and made to pay down the debt.

The wronged person *instinctively* thinks, "I am in pain. Somebody caused this. I must make them pay for my pain so I can find peace again." They open an account for the person who hurt them, begin keeping a record of their wrongs, and look for ways to make them pay for what they did.

Justice exacted on Cain's wrong

After Cain killed Abel in an angry rage, the Lord said to him, "The voice of your brother's blood is crying to Me from the ground. And now you are cursed from the ground, which has opened its mouth to receive your brother's blood from your hands."

Cain paid the price for his unresolved sin against his brother. Living under a curse, he became a vagrant and a wanderer on earth, cut off from the *presence* of his Creator. Thus the law of justice was satisfied.

The law of judgment

The law of judgment says that *the measure we mete out, we will receive back.* What we receive in life is *directly* related to what we have given out. The law of judgment is inescapable–we are dooming ourselves in the same way we are judging others.

For example, when we take a person who wronged us to court, we are seeking a court judgment that will result in justice for us. However, because our desire for justice is criminally greater than the wrongs of our offenders, we become ensnared by our desire to punish. Consider the following Scriptures:

> *Do not judge and you will not be judged; and do not condemn, and you will not be condemned; pardon and you will be pardoned (Luke 6:37).*

> *He who speaks against a brother, or judges his brother, speaks against the law, and judges the law; but if you judge*

the law, you are not a doer of the law, but a judge of it (Jas 4:11-12).

Everyone of you who passes judgment, for in that which you judge another, you condemn yourself (Rom 2:1).

The law of sowing and reaping

The law of sowing and reaping says *we will surely reap what we have sown.* When we judge others, we are sowing a seed which by law someday has to be reaped. Whatever we plant always comes up, even though it can stay underground for many years.

For in the way you judge, you will be judged; and by your standard of measure, it will be measured to you (Matt 7:1-2).

Be not deceived, God is not mocked; for whatsoever a man sows that shall he also reap (Gal 6:7).

They that plow iniquity, and sow wickedness, reap the same (Job 4:8).

The judgmental seed we sow reaps a greater and greater harvest over time, until we confess it and repent of it: "We sow a spark and reap a forest fire." John & Paula Sandford suggest the law of sowing and reaping was meant by God to be a blessing to humanity, not a curse.

Adversity pursues sinners, but the righteous will be rewarded with prosperity (Prov 13:21).

Sow to yourself in righteousness, reap in mercy (Hos 10:12).

The law of honoring parents

The fifth commandment of Moses says that *life will go well for us in every area in which we could, in fact, honor our parents.* The converse can be stated: life will not go well in every area in which we could not honor them.

> *Why do you yourselves transgress the commandment of God ... For God said, 'Honor your father and mother,' and 'whoever speaks evil of father or mother let him be put to death' (Matt 15:4-6).*
>
> *Honor your father and mother (which is the first commandment with a promise), that it may be well with you, and that you may live long on the earth (Eph 6:2-3).*

The Sandfords suggest that failure to honor our parents is at the root of "every marital problem, every child-raising dilemma, and every moral and immoral inclination." Judgments we made against our parents as children will affect our relationships in the future.[29]

Divine Laws Were Never Revoked

God cannot lie (Heb 6:18). His laws are absolute. Every sin[30] demands resolution so the scales of justice will balance.

We like to think that because of grace, God looks the other way or changes his laws. However, He could not do this without violating the essence of who He is—his divine, righteous nature. Jesus confirms this when He said:

> *I did not come to abolish but to fulfill ... until heaven and earth pass away, not the smallest letter or stroke shall pass away from the Law, until all is accomplished (Matt 5:17-19).*

Sin always demands resolution

Until we forgive, the law of retribution will continue to operate. We cannot escape it. Remember what Jesus warned in his parable of the revengeful servant.

> *Then the Lord, moved with anger, handed him over to the torturers until he should repay all that was owed him ... "So shall My heavenly Father also do to you, if each of you does not forgive his brother from your heart" (Matt 18:34-35).*

Jesus also tells us:

> *Make friends quickly with your opponent at law while you are with him on the way, in order that your opponent may not deliver you to the judge, and the judge to the officer, and you be thrown into prison (Matt 5:23-26).*

How Can Balance Be Restored?

When someone offends you, deliberately or ignorantly, what do you do? How do you balance the scales of justice, when you feel like you just got whacked? Here are some ways many of us try.

"I'm sorry" method

If the debtor says "I'm sorry," does this pay down the debt? According to experts, it can—*if* the person speaks from their heart and the offended one receives it. However, they may need to say "I'm sorry" at least four times before the offended one can really hear it and receive it in their heart. (Perhaps by repeating it aloud four times, it may help the offender to drop down into his/her heart and speak from there.)

In saying "I'm sorry" from the heart, the offender is truly acknowledging his/her transgressions (taking responsibility for it, repenting of it, confessing it aloud). Perhaps this is why saying sorry can be efficacious.

Eye for eye method

If your offender will not acknowledge their transgressions against you, or if it is impossible for them to do so, what do you do? Activate the "eye for an eye?" Try to punish them? Make them feel the same pain you felt? Withhold your love? Say hurtful words, emotionally abuse them, or hit them? Do you cut them out of your life?

My favorite way of balancing the scales of justice was to withdraw my emotional presence and not talk to my husband for three days. When I thought he'd been punished enough, then I'd forgive him.

Sweep it under the rug method

Some people use the "sweep it under the rug" method. They try to forget it by pretending it never happened—until such a time as the wound created by the debtor's sin is reactivated and the repressed anger, pain, and hurt come pouring out of it.

> **Note: We are dealing with two things here: 1) the imbalance created by someone's sin/transgression against another; and 2) the wound that was created in the offended one who was sinned against. According to the Scriptures, the wounds created by another person's transgressions against us cannot be healed until we release the transgressor from having to pay down the debt.**

Make sacrifices method

According to the Old Testament, sin automatically brings curses and the penalty of death, just as suspending the law of gravity would cause chaos in the universe. Sacrifices and offerings represented the fulfillment of the penalty for disobedience.

A sin-offering (blood of a young animal) was intended to expiate misdeeds committed through ignorance, forgetfulness, or hastiness (Lev 4:2-3). A guilt-offering was prescribed for transgressions demanding restitution to the victim of the sin (Lev 6:1-7).

Perhaps we try to relieve our guilt over hurting someone by punishing ourselves. Or maybe we do something—charitable work, help somebody in need, go to church more frequently—that helps mollify our guilt feelings.

Do you have a favorite technique to sidestep a forgiveness issue?

God Provides a Better Way

In the Old Testament, God promised to give us a better way to fulfill the law of justice than through the blood of calves and goats:

> *"The days are coming," declares the Lord, "When I will raise up for David a righteous Branch; and He will reign as king and act wisely and do justice and righteousness in the land" (Jer 23:5).*
>
> *And this is the name by which He will be called, "The Lord our righteousness" (Jer 23:5-6).*

Since the earliest of time God has planned a far better way for us to resolve the debts we occur when we cannot fulfill the demands of his righteous law.

> *"Behold, days are coming," declares the LORD, "when I will make a new covenant with the house of Israel and with the house of Judah ... I will put My law within them, and on their heart I will write it ... for I will forgive their iniquity, and their sin I will remember no more" (Jer 31:31-34)*
>
> *But when the fullness of time came, God sent forth His Son, born of a woman, born under the law, in order that He might redeem those who were under the Law (Gal 4:4-5).*

Jesus fulfilled the legal demand of the law

In the New Testament, we are offered a different way to satisfy the demands of the law of justice—through faith in Christ Jesus. In his work on the cross, Jesus was made sin for us.

> *He was pierced through for our transgressions, He was crushed for our iniquities ... the Lord has caused the iniquity of us all to fall on Him (Isa 53:4-6).*

He paid the debt we created by our inability to fulfill the righteous law of God as given to Moses. Jesus died a substitute death for us, paying down the legal debt that we could never pay.

> *... knowing that a man is not justified by the works of the Law but through faith in Christ Jesus (Gal 2:16).*
>
> *... having forgiven us all our transgressions, having cancelled out the certificate of debt consisting of decrees against us and which was hostile to us; and He has taken it out of the way, having nailed it to the cross (Col 2:13-14).*

Presented his blood as an eternal offering

Upon his resurrection, Jesus presented his blood as an eternal offering or sacrifice for our transgressions to the Father—for all time.

> *But when Christ appeared as a high priest of the good things to come ... through His own blood, He entered the holy place once for all, having obtained eternal redemption (Heb 9:11-12).*
>
> *Where there is forgiveness, there is no longer any offering for sin (Heb 10:18).*

Reflection

1. What makes God trustworthy?
2. What is the Law of Justice?
3. Why does every sin demand resolution?

I Forgive You

5

Forgiveness Requires Blood

According to the Law ... all things are cleansed with blood, and without the shedding of blood there is no forgiveness (Heb 9:22)

"Without the Shedding of Blood"

The following Scriptures tell us that transgressions and sins *cannot be forgiven* without blood. It is the shedding of blood that makes forgiveness of our debts possible.

> *For the life is in the blood, and I have given it to you on the altar to make atonement for your souls, for it is the blood by reason of the soul that makes atonement (Lev 17:11).*

> *According to the Law ... all things are cleansed with blood, and without the shedding of blood there is no forgiveness (Heb 9:22).*

God's covenants with humanity require blood

According to the Law of Moses, God required the blood of a sacrificial animal to resolve sin. During the Old Testament period, this blood was accepted as a covering for sin. But it was required yearly because its effectiveness was only temporary.

Even the first covenant was not inaugurated without blood ... Moses took the blood ... and sprinkled both the book itself and all the people, saying, "This is the blood of the covenant which God commanded you" (Heb 9:19-20).

Then through his work on the cross, Jesus Christ gave us another way to pay the debt caused by humanity's transgressions against God's righteous law. Instead of requiring the blood of an animal or the blood of the transgressor, God found a more radical way—the giving of the blood of his only begotten Son. Ponder the following Scriptures:

> *But now apart from the Law, the righteousness of God has been manifested ... whom God displayed publicly as a propitiation [a propitiatory sacrifice] in His blood (Rom 3:21, 25).*
>
> *Now the God of peace, who brought up from the dead the great Shepherd of the sheep through the blood of the eternal covenant, even Jesus our Lord (Heb 13:20).*

Why is blood necessary?

Since ancient times, blood was used as the first ritual sacrament. Later it was symbolized by wine or red ochre. The blood has been symbolic of the seat of the soul and the life force within a person[31]—blood was seen as the carrier of the spirit of life and character that lived in a person.

The importance of blood even today can be seen in our idiomatic expressions: blood money; sweat blood; blood on one's hands; blood out of a stone; blood brother. Perhaps you can think of more.

An eye for an eye—offers a way to get blood

In order to resolve the debt caused by transgressions of the guilty party, we need blood. Without blood, we cannot settle the debt incurred by our transgressor. Where do we get this blood? If we activate the "eye for an eye" method, perhaps we can get the blood.

In going after the transgressor's eye, we are trying to make them bleed internally—psychologically, emotionally, mentally—or even in some situations physically. When we get enough of their blood, then we consider the debt has been paid, the law of justice has been fulfilled.

Jesus gave us a better covenant

Christianity is the only religion that offers us a way to resolve the sin issue—without having to make sacrifices for it or to work for it. It is a free gift given to those who believe. Through faith in Jesus, we can benefit from the blood of Jesus Christ.

> *How much more will the blood of Christ, who through the eternal Spirit offered Himself without blemish to God, cleanse your conscience from dead works to serve the living God (Heb 9:14).*
>
> *In Him we have redemption through His blood, the forgiveness of our trespasses (Eph 1:7).*

Because of the sacrificial blood of Jesus on the cross, God could give us a better way to resolve our sin issue. We can be reconciled with each other, with our self, and with God through the blood of his Son.

> *For the Law [of Moses] made nothing perfect, and on the other hand there is a bringing in of a better hope through which we draw near to God ... Jesus has become the guarantee of a better covenant (Heb 7:19, 22).*
>
> *We have confidence to enter the holy place by the blood of Jesus, by a new and living way which He inaugurated for us ... let us draw near with a sincere heart in full assurance of faith (Heb 10:19-22).*

The Power of the Blood

We need to understand the power of the blood so we can more fully benefit from the blessings it offers us. What is it that makes this blood so powerful?

Life is in the blood

Here's the spiritual reality: the life is in the blood. God established this truth with Noah, and told Moses how to use it in order to resolve the sin issue between the people and Him:

> *To Noah, God said: "You shall not eat flesh with its life, that is, its blood. Surely I will require your lifeblood ... Whoever sheds man's blood, by man his blood shall be shed" (Genesis 9:4-6).*
>
> *God explained to Moses: "The life [soul] of the flesh is in the blood, and I have given it to you on the altar to make atonement for your souls, for it is the blood by reason of the life [soul] that makes atonement ... its blood is identified with its life [soul] (Leviticus 17:11,14).*

Thousands of years later, Jesus affirms the truth that life is in his blood:

> *"Truly, truly, I say to you, unless you eat the flesh of the Son of Man and drink His blood, you have no life in yourselves" (John 6:53).*

The blood of Jesus carries the very life God! This why it is so powerful.

Blessings of the blood

Here are some of the spiritual blessings the blood of Jesus offers us:

1. *Release (redeem, forgive) you from your sins*

> *To Him who ... released us from our sins by His blood (Rev 1:5).*
>
> *In Him we have redemption through His blood, the forgiveness of our trespasses (Eph 1:7).*

2. Cleanse your conscience from guilt

How much more will the blood of Christ ... cleanse science from dead works (Heb 9:14).

3. Justify (vindicate) you

Having now been justified by His blood (Rom 5:9).

4. Free you from futility (unfruitfulness)

You were not redeemed with perishable things like silver and gold from your futile way of life inherited from your forefathers but with precious blood ... the blood of Christ (1 Pet 1:18-19).

5. Overcome your accuser (faultfinder)

They overcame him because of the blood of the Lamb ... (Rev 12:11).

6. Give you peace with God

Through Him, to reconcile all things to Himself, having made peace through the blood of His cross (Col 1:20).

7. Experience the presence of God

Because of the work of Jesus on the cross, we can now be reconciled to God.

Remember that you were at that time separate from Christ ... now in Christ Jesus you who formerly were far off have been brought near by the blood of Christ ... by abolishing in His flesh the enmity, which is the Law of commandments contained in ordinances (Eph 2:12-16).

Through Him to reconcile all things to Himself, having made peace through the blood of His cross (Col 1:20).

We have confidence to enter the holy place by the blood of Jesus (Heb 10:19).

8. Empower you to reign in life

If you have received forgiveness from God for your sins, or given someone else forgiveness, you know first-hand the lightness of spirit it has brought you. Some folks say it feels like a window opened and the room filled with fresh air and light.

St. Paul expresses the power of forgiveness on our lives like this: "Those who receive the abundance of grace and of the gift of righteousness will reign in life through the One, Jesus Christ" (Rom 5:17).

We express the power of the blood in the hymns we love to sing:

- *What can wash away my sin? Nothing but the blood of Jesus*
- *Redeemed, redeemed, redeemed by the blood of the lamb*
- *Would you be free from the burden of sin? . . . There is power, power, wonder-working power in the blood of the Lamb*
- *There is a fountain filled with blood, drawn from Immanuel's veins; and sinners plunged beneath that flood, lose all their guilty stains*

Through faith we partake of his blood

Jesus gave us his blood and told us to partake of it: "Drink from it, all of you; for this is My blood of the covenant, which is poured out for many for forgiveness of sins" (Matt 26:27-28).

St. Paul helps the early believers to understand this when he asked: "Is not the cup of blessing which we bless a sharing in the blood of Christ" (1 Cor 10:16)? But in order to benefit from the blood we must apply faith when we partake of the Eucharist or Communion.

Experience a growing freedom

The sacrificial blood of Christ was given so we can resolve the debts created by the wrongs committed against us. His blood alone has the power to set us free from deep-seated resentment, smoldering anger, and bitterness, enabling us to keep our hearts open and let the love of God flow to others.

If you understand and use the blood of Jesus to empower you to forgive all others, including yourself, you will experience a growing freedom within you. You will experience answered prayers. Your wounds can begin to heal. And the enemy will not have the right to torment you.

> *How much severer punishment do you think he will deserve who has trampled underfoot the Son of God, and has regarded as unclean the blood of the covenant, by which he was sanctified, and has insulted the Spirit of grace. ... 'Vengeance is Mine, I will repay' (Heb 10:29-30).*

If you have been saved from the wrath of God through Christ Jesus, then why would you make someone else live under your judgment and wrath?

> *Much more then, having now been justified by [in] His blood, we shall be saved from the wrath of God through Him (Rom 5:9).*

We no longer need to use the "eye for an eye" method or to try harder to meet the demands of the righteous law of God. We can go to Jesus Christ.

Rejecting the Blood of Jesus

Christ provided a way for us to resolve the debts we cannot pay. We no longer need to damage our capacity to be at peace with others or our self because of a guilty conscience. Through forgiveness we can be freed.

Must avail ourselves of the blood of Christ

However, we will not automatically benefit from the blood of Jesus if we do not avail ourselves of it. If we do not take responsibility for our failures, stop blaming others, confess our sins, and receive forgiveness, we will reap in full—despite the mercy and grace God made available to us.

Many people in their ignorance fail to release others from their debts. They do not know God's peace, joy, and righteousness in their hearts. They fail to connect their unforgiveness to their problems and difficulties.

Neither do they benefit from the power of the blood of Jesus to cleanse their guilty consciences. Moreover, they do not understand that God has given them the blood so they can forgive even their worst debtors. Instead they reject the blood of Jesus as not enough for their sins or the sins of others.

"Your blood is not enough"

When we refuse to forgive those who hurt us, we are saying, "Sorry, Jesus, Your blood sacrifice is not enough for me. I must do it myself!"

For years I did this. I had a problem with forgiving my husband. When I was hurt, I withdrew from him, not speaking to him for several days. After I'd punished him enough, then I would forgive him.

One day when stuck in my anger, the Holy Spirit made me aware I was rejecting the blood of Jesus Christ as not enough for the sins of my husband. This revelation freed me from trying to make him pay for how he'd hurt me. Jesus had already paid down the debt and offered me his blood.

Healing power of the blood of Jesus

Traumas often leave negative pictures in our minds, sometimes tormenting us for many years afterwards. Perhaps the neurons of the brain get stuck at the point of shock, and our brain won't let us move on. Or perhaps a demonic spirit fastened itself to us in the moment of the trauma. Either way, Jesus Christ offers us his blood as a way to resolve these traumas. Here are two encounters with his blood.

> **A chalice of blood frees me**
>
> Some years ago I experienced the power of the blood of Jesus in a dramatic way. After discovering some porn pictures under a bed, I could not erase them from my mind. So I went to Jesus and told Him how these pictures were disturbing me.
>
> As I prayed, I saw in the eye of my spirit, a chalice of blood being poured down upon the pictures. As the blood spread out across the pictures, it formed the shape of a cross. I was freed. The torment instantly left.
>
> **"Go, take my blood"**
>
> A friend in northern Germany felt God wanted her to go back to Poland, where she had seen horrific wrongs as a 12-year-old living in a camp following WWII. However, the vivid memories of the innocent blood shed in the streets were too painful for her to return.
>
> She went to Jesus, shared her pain with Him, then heard the voice of the Lord say to her, "Go and take My blood with you. My blood is enough for the wrongs that you saw there." She was freed to do what Jesus wanted her to and as a result she became a healing vessel for some people in that city.

Reflection

1. How can the blood of Jesus help people forgive?
2. What makes the blood of Jesus so powerful?
3. How have you benefited from the blood of Jesus?

I Forgive You

6

What Is Forgiveness?

The lord of that servant felt compassion and released him and forgave him the debt (Matt 18:27).

In the Lord's Prayer, Jesus teaches us to pray: "Forgive us our debts, as we also have forgiven our debtors" (Matt 6:12). In the Gospel of Mark, He says, "Whenever you stand praying, forgive, if you have anything against anyone; so that your Father also who is in heaven may forgive you your transgressions" (Mark 11:26).

Sin creates a debt

What is it we are to forgive? We are to forgive *the debt.* Jesus is saying that when someone transgresses or sins[32] against us, a debt has been created and needs to be resolved—and He *expects us to settle that debt* which was created by our transgressor. He is asking us to release the person from having to pay down their debt. He says we can do this through forgiveness!

Remember, the law of justice requires the one who committed the wrong to be held accountable and made to pay down the debt in order to balance the scales of justice.

When someone violates the law of justice—through transgressions, deliberately or ignorantly—an account has been opened, a debt has been created, and an imbalance has resulted. To restore balance (harmony), the debt *must* be paid down by someone, i.e., justified. There is no other way! The debt incurred when someone violates the law of justice must be resolved.

> *For indeed what I have forgiven ... I did it for your sakes ... that no advantage be taken of us by Satan; for we are not ignorant of his schemes* (2 Cor 2:10-11).

To do what Jesus says, we need to understand what is meant by biblical forgiveness.

Defining Forgiveness

In Matt 18:27, Jesus said, "The lord of that servant felt compassion and released him and forgave [*aphiemi*] him the debt." The Greek word *aphiemi* translated "forgave," means "to dismiss, to cut off, to release" something.

In this biblical story, the lord felt compassion and cut off the indebtedness of the servant; i.e., he dismissed the debt that the servant owed him. The servant was no longer responsible to pay it.

Forgiving the debt, not the person

Notice this vital distinction: the focus of forgiveness is on the *debt*, not the person who owed the debt. It is the debt that receives the action of the verb "forgive."

When the lord dismissed the debt, cutting it off, the debt no longer existed; it was wiped out. When we ask the Lord to forgive us our transgressions, our sins, we are asking Him to dismiss the debt we owe, not dismiss us.[33]

Dictionary definition

The dictionary defines "forgive" like this: 1) to grant pardon for or remission of an offense or debt; absolve; 2) to give up all claim on account of; to remit a debt or obligation; 3) to grant pardon to a person; 4) to cease to feel resentment against someone; 5) to cancel an indebtedness or liability of. Notice the emphasis on the debt agrees with the Greek definition.

Clinical definitions

Here are definitions of forgiveness by people in the helping professions:

- A freely made intention to let go of the bitter debt to which we hold another. It is a desire to let go that grows out of a commitment to free oneself and the other person from the bondage of debt and hurt, however grievous (Harry Aponte).[34]
- A willingness to abandon one's right to resentment, negative judgment, and indifferent behavior toward one who unjustly injured us, while fostering the underserved qualities of compassion, generosity, and even love toward him or her (R.D. Enright & Rique).[35]
- The intentional replacement of the "Will to Punish" those who harm with the "Will to Forgive." Forgiveness is an exercise of free will, conducted before the face of God, with the formal intention to abandon the pursuit of equal harm to the harmer. Forgiveness is grounded fully in the ego of the forgiver and results in healing psychological complexes outside the ego's control through the power of the Holy Spirit in the name of Jesus Christ (Charles L. Zeiders).[36]

Aspects of Biblical Forgiveness

(The ideas presented in this section are drawn from Zeiders, Enright,[37] Caine & Kaufman,[38] Smith,[39] Anderson, [40] and Dayton.[41])

Following is a description of characteristics that are at the heart of biblical forgiveness.

1. A decision to obey the Lord

Forgiveness is motivated by obedience to the Lord. Since Jesus tells us to forgive, it is something we *can* do. We can make a decision to release someone from our retaliation right now.

Biblical forgiveness does not ask us to wait until we feel like it. We are instructed to forgive our debtors, whenever we stand before the Lord and make our petitions before Him.

> **You say, "You don't understand how much this person hurt me!" But don't you see, they are still hurting you! How do you stop the pain? You don't forgive someone for their sake; you do it for your own sake so you can be free. Your need to forgive isn't an issue between you and the offender; it's between you and God (Unknown).**

The Spirit of God dwelling in you gives you the ability to think like your Father, act like your Father, talk like your Father, and forgive like your Father, whether you feel like it or not. God does not wait until He feels like it to forgive us. Do you think Jesus felt like forgiving while He was on the cross?

A choice we make

God has provided us with the blood we need in order to forgive. If we choose not to forgive, we are saying to the Lord that we will not accept his blood as enough for the sins of our transgressors.

Dr. Ed Smith warns us not to say, "Lord, please help me to forgive," because he is already helping you. Do not say, "Lord, I want to forgive," because you are bypassing the hard-core choices that are your responsibility. Rather say, "Lord, I choose to forgive."

2. Something we do for ourselves

Earlier we looked at the high cost of unforgiveness, so we can understand why the Lord wants us forgive the people who injured us. We suggest that it is out of concern for our well-being that He commands us to forgive. He says if we do not forgive our debtors from the heart, God will not forgive us—*and* we will be turned over to the torturers.

3. Benefits us more than the one we forgive

In choosing to forgive our debtors, we are the ones who will gain the most, not them. When we forgive them, releasing them from their debt to us, then we are released from that burden in our lives. Unless they humble themselves, take responsibility for their transgressions, repent, and turn to the Lord, nothing will have changed for the debtor. They are still the same person.

4. Surrender our right to get even

Biblical forgiveness requires something far more than obedience; it requires us to surrender our right to get even with the person who wronged us. It is possible to think we have forgiven, but never let go of the debt—we never released the other person from retaliation.

Letting go requires us to apply some faith in our heart, some confidence and assurance as we let go of what was owed us, and surrender ourselves into the hands of a loving God who cares for us.

When we want to take our own revenge, we are setting ourselves up as God. In Romans we are instructed to not pay back evil for evil to anyone or to take our own revenge:

> *Leave room for the wrath of God, for it is written, 'Vengeance is Mine, I will repay,' says the Lord (Rom 12:19).*

5. Releases us from the past

Our feelings of resentment, hatred, anger, and desire for revenge are destructive emotions that do us great harm, actually holding us in bondage to the past. These negative feelings will continue to rob us of our God-given creative energy that enables us to live life more creatively and fully. Until we forgive our transgressors, our energy will be tied up with these destructive emotions. We will be held in bondage to them.

Biblical forgiveness releases us from the people who wounded us and frees us from our painful past. We are now able to move forward in our lives.

6. Agree to live with effects of transgressor's sin

Sin always costs something. In biblical forgiveness we agree to live with the results of the sin of our transgressor—but in freedom instead of bitterness. Here are thoughts from Dr. Neil Anderson that give us a key to doing the hard work of forgiveness.

Forgiveness is costly. Jesus took the consequences of our sins upon Himself. All true forgiveness is substitutionary, because no one really forgives without bearing the consequences of the other person's sin. God the Father "made Him who knew no sin to be sin on our behalf, that we might become the righteousness of God in Him" (2 Cor 5:21).

Where is the justice? It is the cross that makes forgiveness legally and morally right: "For the death that He died, He died to sin, once for all" (Ro 6:10).[42]

7. Happens internally in the heart

Biblical forgiveness must come from the heart. The heart must be postured with a "will to forgive," in order to give a merciful response to one who hurt us.

> *The Lord looks on the heart (I Sa 14:7).*
>
> *... if each of you does not forgive his brother from your heart (Matt. 18:35).*

How do you forgive from your heart? You acknowledge the hurt and the hate. If your forgiveness does not visit the emotional core of your life, it will be incomplete.

Many feel the pain of interpersonal offenses but they won't, or don't know how to, acknowledge it. Let God bring the pain to the surface so He can deal with it—this is where the healing takes place.

8. Calls for our courage

Many people think forgiveness is for the weak, so they choose to carry others' transgressions in the bitterness of unforgiveness inside of them. However, forgiveness requires courageous people who are willing to confront their pain, accept themselves as permanently changed, and make difficult choices. Then they can live in the freedom that forgiveness brings them.

> **Countless individual are satisfied to go on resenting and hating people who wrong them. They stew in their own inner poisons and even contaminate those around them. Forgivers, on the other hand, are not content to be stuck in a quagmire. They reject the possibility that the rest of their lives will be determined by the unjust and injurious acts of another—Beverly Flanigan.**[43]

9. A choice, not manipulated by pressure

Years ago I witnessed an abuse of power by a clergy. We (patients & staff) were watching a film on sexual abuse, when a few patients began to curl up in pain sobbing. The room hushed. The other patients were quietly present and compassionate. Then the resident clergy spoke up, telling them that they needed to forgive their abusers. The room exploded in anger. "No!" the patients called out.

We need to have a compassionate heart when we help people—to weep with those who weep. To be with them while they remember the wrongs committed against them. To witness their pain. To help them make an account of the wrongs they have suffered. To understand what the sins of others have cost them. Remember, Jesus healed people out of compassion—not judgment.

10. Embrace a new way of thinking

Even though some things don't change on the outside, because of Jesus Christ we have the power to change how we think about things on the inside. Biblical forgiveness involves embracing a new way of thinking about the people who transgressed against us.

> *I say to you, love your enemies, and pray for those who persecute you (Matt 5:44).*
>
> *Father forgive them; for they do not know what they are doing (Luke 23:34).*

Reflection

1. Compare the definitions of forgiveness with your notion of what it is.
2. When you forgive someone, what are you forgiving: the person or the debt?
3. What motivates you to forgive another person?

7

Misconceptions About Forgiveness

Peter came and said to Him, 'Lord, how often shall my brother sin against me and I forgive him. Up to seven times?' (Matt 18:21-22).

There are many commonly held misconceptions about what forgiveness is. Inaccurate ideas confuse and actually hinder us from doing what Jesus said. To help us clear up our misunderstandings, we will first explore what forgiveness is not.[44]

Forgiveness Is Not ...

1. Forgiveness is not dependent upon the offender

Forgiveness does not depend upon whether your offenders want or ask for it. It does not matter whether or not they were sorry for it. It involves only your cutting off the debt that their offense created. If you forgive your debtor their indebtedness, you will no longer hold them accountable to pay for what they did.

2. Forgiveness is not something we do for our offender

Forgiveness is not about fulfilling an obligation or duty to our offender. We do not forgive because we owe them, nor do we forgive for their sake. We forgive because Jesus told us to.

3. Forgiveness is not about going to our offender

Many people mistakenly think forgiveness is about going to their offender, but biblical forgiveness does not require this. In fact, it may even be harmful—they may be unaware, or if aware, thought it already was forgiven. They may even be dead.

You must be led by the Holy Spirit in this. You also need to examine your reasons for going. After you've done the hard work of forgiveness, the Holy Spirit may nudge you to go, possibly for reconciliation, but you must wait for his timing and wisdom.

> **God guides me through a dream**
>
> As leader of a women's ministry, I'd become friends with a prestigious woman speaker and often traveled with her. Then she became offended with me because we wouldn't join her church, and she began to speak negatively about me to others. Not knowing what to do, I asked the Lord. That night, I dreamed:
>
> I'm in a meeting, and the offering is being taken. A voice says, "Give me something from your purse." I look in my purse and see a needle & thread and a magnifying glass. I put them in the offering basket.
>
> When I awoke, I knew that I wasn't to try to mend our relationship, and I was not to focus on it or magnify it.

4. Forgiveness isn't about condoning wrong behavior

Forgiveness requires you to recognize that something wrong occurred, but it does not ask you to sanction or condone the sinful behavior of your offender.

5. Forgiveness is not about denial

Another mistaken notion says that if we deny the unjust offense, pretending it never happened, then we have forgiven. No! Pushing it down under, denying the pain, does not resolve the debt.

As Christians we tend to pretend that something did not hurt us, perhaps because of pride—but we deceive ourselves. Denying the offense only creates more problems for us in the future. We swallow the emotion, taking it deep inside, where it can do damage to our bodies later in life.

6. Forgiveness is not about trying to change the offender

Forgiveness is not a means of changing another person but rather the avenue of release for you—the person who was hurt. We do not forgive someone because we hope it will change them. Don't fall into the trap of believing that if you forgive the person, it will cause them to change. Not true!

Beware of using forgiveness as a way to manipulate someone. Also, don't deceive yourself into believing that your offender has been touched by God or that reconciliation is now possible. Real forgiveness says, "I forgive you regardless of whether you change."

Forgiveness has the power to change only you, not your offender. It releases you from the bondage that enslaves you because you are holding the note of the debt—but it may not impact the offender. It is a lie that other people's behavior has the power to control your emotions and thoughts.

7. Forgiveness is not about trying to forget

Another belief says, if we can forget what happened then we have forgiven. In fact, most people who try to forget discover that it doesn't work. However, we may find that once we truly forgive someone, the offense seems to fade away in our minds.

God says He will "remember our sins no more" (Heb 10:17), but God, being omniscient, cannot forget. "Remember our sins no more" means that God will never use the past against us (Ps 103:12). Forgetting may be the result of forgiveness, but it is never the *means* of forgiveness. When we bring up the past against others, we are saying we haven't forgiven them.

8. Forgiveness is not about restoring relationship

It does not have to do with restoring a relationship or making things right between you and your offender. Don't forget: forgiveness is focused on the *debt*—not the debtor. It has to do with the removal or release of an indebtedness, but *nothing to do with restoring a relationship*. It is the transgressor's unjust *behavior* that receives the action of the verb "forgive," not the *person*.

Dr. Charles Zeiders says, "One's forgiveness does not necessarily heal or influence the other person. Human nature is fallen, and people are capable of sadism, abuse, and grotesque behaviors that will again hurt us."[45] Jesus knows this truth. In Matt 10:17, He warns, "Be on your guard against men."

Forgiveness is not about fulfilling an obligation or duty to the person who hurt you. You do not forgive because you owe the person something, nor do it for their sake. You forgive because Jesus told us to.

9. Forgiveness is not about trying to hold on to someone

Closely linked to the above is the idea that if we forgive our debtors then they will not abandon, reject, or desert us. Many physically and emotionally abused people continu-

ally forgive their violent partner out of fe
Cowards, they prefer to live with their al
break free from them.

They are naïve in thinking that they
partner through forgiveness. We need to understand that, because we carry the corrupted seed from Adam, people are capable of all manner of degradation and evil.

Common sense warns us not to ignore what we've learned about human nature. If you've been hurt by someone, keep your distance from them. Don't assume just because you forgave them that they've changed.

Actually forgiveness is a way for you to break free from being held in bondage to your debtors. Forgiving them frees you from trying to get something from them.

10. Forgiveness is never conditional

Forgiving debtors is never conditional. Don't say, "I'll forgive you, *if* you do this or that." If so, then you are still trying to make them pay down the debt they owe you. Once you forgive their debt, they do not owe you anything.

Forgiveness Is Not Reconciliation

Many people have the mistaken idea that forgiveness is the same as reconciliation. This is far from the truth! Forgiveness and reconciliation are two very separate actions.

Forgiveness has to do with the removal or release of a debt; *reconciliation* has to do with restoring friendship or harmony between two people, i.e., repairing a broken relationship. For true reconciliation to take place, something must take place in the heart or spirit of both you and your offender.

Thoughts by professional counselors

- Reconciliation is the offender's responsibility and occurs when the offender recognizes his or her wrong and takes actions to correct the offending behavior (Freedman & Enright).
- For reconciliation to take place, some groundwork must take place. Some type of event must happen in the spirit of each person, the offender and the offended. This creates opportunities for reconciliation of the people (Unknown).
- Because reconciliation has to do with resuming the relationship, it carries complex considerations about the nature of the bond between people, whether of blood, marriage, or friendship. The obligation towards a child, for example, carries a different expectation from a friendship. Reconciliation also raises questions about depth of attachment and the risk of further hurt.
- How much are people prepared to put up with to be with someone they love? My notion of love in forgiveness does not hold reconciliation to be universally required for every relationship. Forgiveness is always possible, while not all relationships continue to be viable (Harry Aponte).
- Note holders can forgive their offender, but they cannot reconcile the offender to themselves unless the offender cooperates. Reconciliation requires the offenders to come to the place where they are willing to confess the error of their way. Along with this confession, the offender must give evidence of genuine brokenness and a contrite heart, seek restoration and restitution. If the offender does not admit his or her wrong and accept full responsibility for it, reconciliation is not possible (Ed Smith).

Reconciliation requires God's guidance

When it comes to reconciliation, we must be led by the Spirit of God, otherwise we might make things worse. We must go to the Lord and ask for his wisdom and knowledge about how to handle our different situations. Sometimes there may be a timing involved, or perhaps the Lord might not want us to try and fix the broken relationship, for reasons we know not.

We are instructed to "Be at peace with others as far as we are able" (Rom 12:18). But apparently there are situations in which it is not possible.

> **"Take him back"**
>
> **Years ago a co-worker decided he no longer wanted to work alongside us. A few months later, he changed his mind and wanted to come back. A friend exerted pressure on me to take the man back. Feeling unsure, I went to the Lord for direction.**
>
> **As I opened the Bible, my eyes fell on Acts 15:37-40 and I read: "Barnabas was desirous of taking John, called Mark, along with them also. But Paul kept insisting that they should not take him along who had deserted them in Pamphylia ... There arose such a sharp disagreement that they separated from one another, and Barnabas took Mark with him and sailed away to Cyprus."**
>
> **I knew how the Lord wanted me to handle this: No, I was not to take the co-worker back.**

Remember, forgiveness is focused on the debt (unjust offense), not the debtor (offender). The power to forgive lies totally in the hands of the one who holds the note of debt. But reconciliation is a completely different matter. Confusing these two spiritual realities results in many problems.

Reflection

1. Which of the mistaken beliefs are you familiar with?
2. Why may reconciliation not be good for someone?
3. Be alert to how God may use dreams to help you work through areas of unforgiveness.

8

Pathway to Heart-Based Forgiveness

Not with eye service, as men pleasers; but as servants of Christ, doing the will of God from the heart (Eph 6:6).

The parable of the unforgiving servant helps us to understand what is involved in forgiving from the heart (see Matt 18:21-35).

Jesus tells about a king's servant who was forgiven his substantial debt by the king, but refused to forgive his friend who owed him a small amount of money. This angered the king, who then handed his servant over to torturers. Jesus warns that a similar fate can befall anyone who refuses to forgive others from the heart.

The pathway to heart-based forgiveness demands that something take place deep inside us. We can't just give mental agreement and then brush it away as unimportant. To be real, forgiveness must touch our heart in some significant way. We no longer demand that the person suffer the way they have made us suffer.

Become Aware

To forgive from the heart often requires that some ground work be done. In the parable by Jesus, the king wanted to settle accounts, so he had to find out what was owed him.

The kingdom of heaven may be compared to a certain king who wished to settle accounts with his slaves and when he began to settle them, there was brought to him one who owed him ten thousand talents (Matt 18:23-24).

1. Aware of your need

Forgiveness is usually motivated by an awareness that you are hurting in some way or that you are continually recalling the failures of some individual and sharing them with others. This awareness enables us to acknowledge that our mind or heart is not at peace with someone.

Sometimes you may not be aware that you are holding an offense until the Holy Spirit makes you aware of it. This awareness may occur suddenly, but other times it may be gradual.

2. Acknowledge you have been sinned against

Forgiveness requires you to acknowledge that you have been hurt by another person's sin or transgression. This may be hard. You know you are hurting, but you are not sure why—you think perhaps it is your fault.

Some people don't trust their own perception of some event, because they were taught as children not to. They were told over and over that what they were seeing wasn't true—when it was.

Acknowledging sin brings freedom

Many years ago a friend was telling us how much he was hurting, and no matter how much he prayed about it, the pain wouldn't go away. He even went to a Christian therapist for help, but to no avail. As we listened to his story of how he was hurt, I suddenly said to him, "You were sinned against, weren't you?"

He looked astonished. His countenance brightened up. He had not considered that his painful feelings were a

consequence of being sinned against. Later, he told us how much this one thought helped him and he was free of the pain.

Other people try to pretend that something did not hurt them, perhaps because of pride. But the truth is that they are deceiving themselves. Denying their painful response only creates more problems for them in the future. They swallow their emotion, taking it deep inside, where it can do much greater damage to them later in life.

3. Take an account of what happened

The next step is to take an accurate account of what happened. Before you can cut off or dismiss a debt, it is necessary to know exactly what was done or not done, and the extent of the damage. In the parable of Jesus, the king needed to know what the servant owed him.

Know what you need to forgive the offender for

Identify exactly what they did or failed to do for you. What was their sin against you? What do you need to forgive them for?

For example: I needed to forgive my mom for not saying she loved me before she died.

Identify what their sin cost you

Identify exactly what their sin cost you, the price you pay because of their unjust action. What do they owe you? What did you want from them?

For example: My Mother's failure to use my name and say she loved me before she died hurt me. I wanted her to recognize me as an individual, separate from my sister and my brothers. I wanted her to affirm me, to bless me as her daughter, before she died, but she was unable to do it.

Become Honest

True forgiveness requires psychological and emotional honesty with our self and with God. We must not only acknowledge the truth about what happened but also our feelings of hurt, resentment, vengeance, and anger. These destructive emotions must become available to us. Otherwise, our forgiveness may take place only in our mind, not in our heart.[46]

We need to take the time, not rush our forgiveness. If our forgiveness does not visit the emotional core of our life, it will be incomplete.

> *When the king came to realize the seriousness of the situation, he reacted with anger. He commanded the servant to be sold into slavery with his wife & children until he could repay his debt (Matt 18:34).*

4. Identify how their sin made you feel

Identify exactly how their sin made you feel. What feelings did you experience as a result of their transgression against you? Many feel the pain of interpersonal offenses, but they don't have the courage or know how to acknowledge it. If you are unable to access your pain, ask the Lord to bring you in touch with it.

Did you feel abandoned, rejected, unwanted, unloved, or left out? Were you afraid, anxious, worried, or terrified? What about embarrassed, ashamed, bad, blamed, or stupid? Belittled, betrayed, unloved, or deceived? Angry, resentful, enraged?

For example: I felt sad, disappointed, unimportant, and frustrated (anger-based) when my Mother couldn't say "I love *you*" before she died.

5. Anger must be acknowledged and released

Although our typical response to injustice is to get angry, we must acknowledge and release the anger before freedom will come.

In the parable of the unforgiving servant, the king became angry; his first reaction was to take revenge and punish the servant. Anger was a very healthy response to this apparently totally irresponsible behavior. How could his servant have ever gotten so deeply in debt? But the King realized that the money was gone and he would never get it back.

Anger is an emotion for which the Christian community has little tolerance—it is seen as a sin and unbecoming. Many families also taught this belief. If you get angry, you are often scolded and shamed. But the Bible tells us to *be angry and don't sin*: "Don't let the sun go down on your anger or you will give the devil an opportunity" (Eph 4:26).

The length of time you hold on to anger, and what you do with it, has much to do with whether it becomes sin or not. I hold that we must not be too quick to tell someone to forgive, especially if they are not yet in touch with their pain and anger.

Satan wants us to dwell on anger and do nothing about it. He wants us to turn the anger inward and bury it deeply. So demonic forces will take the opportunity to stir up this old anger and we will express old anger in a new situation.

Expressing old anger never depletes it. Until the anger is expressed and released by the Lord Jesus, we are destined to perpetually dump it on whoever happens to trigger it.[47]

Make a Decision

As we discussed earlier, we must make a decision to release our desire to even the score and instead forgive the offender.

We can't wait until we *feel* like it—we might never get there. Accepting the blood of Jesus as enough for the sins of our debtor frees us to decide we will forgive them.

Our decision to forgive involves giving up our right to negatively judge someone who has wounded us and instead extend compassion toward them. This reflects our commitment to release our self and the other person from any burden of debt and injury.

> *Since he did not have the means to repay, his Lord commanded him to be sold, along with his wife and children and all that he had, and repayment to be paid (Matt 18:25).*
>
> *The slave therefore falling down, prostrated himself before him saying, "Have patience with me, and I will repay you everything" (Matt 18:26).*

6. Recognize your debtor is unable to repay the debt

When the servant begged for forgiveness, the king realized that he'd never have the means to repay the debt. We also come to the same point where we realize that our offender does not have the means to repay their debt.

When we are hurt, we look to the person who hurt us for repayment. We want to make them pay for our loss, thinking it will take away our pain. But in most cases, they do not have the power (resources) to do this. They might even be dead.

Only Jesus has the power to take away our pain and heal our wounds. He is the only one who can pay back and restore the debt of the losses we have incurred in our lives.

Does apologizing help?

Most people say they feel better after receiving an apology from the person who hurt them. According to Dr. Everett L. Worthington, "If someone apologizes, it makes it easier to give some measure of forgiveness because it reduces the gap of injustice."[48] But it seems the offender needs to apologize at least four times, because it takes that long to open the wounded person's heart and receive it.

7. Stop demanding your debtor change

At this point, we stop all demands that the one who hurt us must change. Forgiveness is never a means of changing someone else, but rather the avenue of release for us. We do not say, "I'll forgive you, *if* you do this or that." If so, then we are still trying to make our transgressor pay down the debt they owe us. Once we forgive them, they owe us nothing.

8. Disconnect transgressor from their sin

Forgiveness becomes easier for you if you can separate your offender from their sins. They are not your enemy; it is their sins that are your enemy. When you make their sin equal to them, you not only hate what they did, but also hate the person who did the sin.

When God saved us, He separated us from our sin. He saw our sin, but He saw *us* without it. He loved us even in our sin, because He was able to separate us from our sin. This means that we too can forgive others of their failures, yet love them.

9. Agree to live with consequences of your transgressor's sin

In forgiving others, you are agreeing to live with the consequences of their sins, but in the freedom of forgiveness, rather than in the bitterness of unforgiveness. This is why you need to do some ground work: Do you know how their sin has affected you? The price you paid for it? What did it cost you? What did you lose?

Suppose a drunk driver hits your car; you are injured and your child is killed. You will live with the consequences of that driver's sin for the rest of your life—you will pay the price for their sin, whether you want to or not.

This is why, when we come to forgive, we need to understand exactly what the unjust action was and what it cost us. What did we lose because of that person's sin against us?

Note: If someone is too quick to forgive, and their pain or anger is not available to them, they are probably in denial. Before doing the hard work of forgiveness, it may be better to wait until they are in touch with their anger.[49]

Begin Forgiving

Here we begin the active work of forgiving. Through an act of our will before God in prayer, we assert our *Will to Forgive* over our *Will to Punish* our debtor,[50] and we surrender our right to get even.

Some type of spiritual event takes place in our heart that empowers us to release our transgressor from their debt. The evidence of heart-based forgiveness is compassion.

> *And the lord of that slave felt compassion and released him and forgave him the debt (Matt 18:27).*
>
> *Should you not also have had mercy on your fellow slave, even as I had mercy on you? (Matt 18:33).*
>
> *So shall My heavenly Father also do to you if each of you does not forgive his brother from your heart (Matt 18:35).*

10. Release your debtor from their debt

In forgiving your transgressor, you are dismissing the debt they owe you. You are saying, "I no longer require you to suffer the way you made me suffer."

In releasing our debtors, we are free of the anger and the stresses of maintaining the note of debt. This requires us to apply some faith, some confidence and assurance in our heart, that as we let go of what was owed us and surrender it into God's hands, He has taken responsibility for it.

11. Allow your emotional core to be touched

In the parable of Jesus, the king is *feeling* something that allows him to freely release the servant of the debt. The feeling of "compassion" exposes the true heart of the king.

Compassion is the benevolent emotion we express toward another with whom we have made some inner identification. It says *I know the pain you carry, for I also have carried a similar burden.* Feeling compassion can ease the hard work of forgiveness in a way that nothing else can.

When you are willing to revisit the hurt caused by your transgressor and go to the Lord with your pain, you typically experience empathy and compassion for the one who hurt you.

Undergo change in your heart

Forgiveness is a merciful response from our heart to someone who has unjustly hurt us. This is possible when we see our offender in a new light. We get a new picture of a needy, weak, complicated, and fallible human being like us. As a result, we experience a radical change in our heart.

Biblical forgiveness requires that something takes place in our heart. This is the crucial moment in forgiving others. Once we see that every human being has inherited a corrupted seed from Adam, blame dies.

It was the nature of Jesus to forgive, and when we receive Him into our hearts, we receive his nature—loving and forgiving. The same spirit that was in Jesus is in us too, so we also are able to forgive. Real forgiveness is the giving of the love of Christ through the Holy Spirit to one who needs it.

> *Be merciful, just as your Father is merciful (Luke 6:36-37).*
>
> *Jesus said, "Father, forgive them, for they do not know what they are doing" (Luke 23:3).*

12. Stop speaking evil against offender & wish them well

When you speak evil against someone by citing the wrong committed against you, it activates the law of judgment. You must decide instead that you will bear the burden of someone's transgression by not using it against them in the future. Forgive them and bless them.

> *Everyone of you who passes judgment, for in that which you judge another, you condemn yourself (Rom 2:1).*

Although there may be times when someone is required to testify for the sake of justice, it should not be for the purpose of seeking revenge from a bitter heart.

Reflection

1. Identify the most important or most challenging of the 12 steps.
2. How might compassion empower us to forgive our offenders?
3. Why is it important to stop speaking evil against our offenders?

9

Bedrock Truths of Christianity

Repent, and let each of you be baptized in the name of Jesus Christ for the forgiveness of your sins (Acts 2:38).

If you grew up in a Christian environment, you may have become word-hardened to the bedrock truths of Christianity or perhaps never really understood them—sin, repentance, faith.

And of course you're going to say, "I know what they mean!" But please take a moment and briefly review the basic meaning of these foundational spiritual concepts. They will empower you in doing the hard work of forgiving.

1. What Is Sin?

Growing up in church, I developed my understanding of sin under the fiery preaching of our pastor. Sin was tainted with the idea that I was bad. It took years of walking with the Lord before I understood that *I* was not bad, but instead it was *sin* which dwells in my flesh. (See Rom 7:17-21).

Missing the mark

Most of us usually think of sin as something that causes us to feel condemned or that we are bad; however, in the Hebrew and Greek it lacked this quality.

In the Old Testament, the Hebrew word *chatah* usually translated as *sin*, actually means "to miss" (the road).

In the New Testament, the Greek word *harmartia*, translated *sin*, means to "miss the mark." Both of these words lack the quality of condemnation which the words sin and sinner have been endowed with over time.

> *For all have sinned [hamartano] and come short of the glory of God (Rom 3:23).*

So we can say that "sin" simply means that we *missed the mark*. The question is: what was the *mark* that we missed?

The royal law

Jesus Christ explains his understanding in the Gospel of Matthew:

> *Therefore, however you want people to treat you, so treat them, for this is the Law and the Prophets (Matt 7:12)*

In the Epistles, St. James gives us examples of how we can miss the royal law:

> *If, however, you are fulfilling the royal law according to the Scripture, "You shall love your neighbor as yourself," you are doing well. But if you show partiality, you are committing sin and are convicted by the law as transgressors (Jas 2:8-9).*

> *Therefore to one who knows the right thing to do, and does not do it, to him it is sin (Jas 4:17).*

How often have you said something you regret? Behaved in some way because you wanted to look good? Respected certain people, but not others? Perhaps you see how easily we can sin against someone and cause them pain.

Sin always hurts

As already explained, heart-based forgiveness necessitates admitting that we felt hurt by something. We may find this difficult because we don't understand that what happened was sin. After all, we are not God. Who are we to say someone sinned?

We confuse hurt with sin, failing to recognize that what happened was a result of someone's sin. We need to know that sin always hurts, to some degree or another. The truth is that we are hurting because of someone's sin.

As children, we may have been afraid to think our parents sinned against us, because it might mean that they didn't love us or we'd lose their love. So we'd rather think it was our fault and swallow our pain. Later it grows into a root of bitterness which can only by removed through heart-based forgiveness.

Understanding what sin is enables us to take a more accurate account of what actually happened or did not happen to us. Calling it sin makes it easier for us forgive, because we know that Jesus died for our sins and gave us his blood so we could forgive the debt of the people who sin against us.

Is unforgiveness sin?

If we deny our pain and fail to forgive, is this sin? Is it sin if you hold grudges, recite your list of wrongs, or demand justice when you've been wronged? Is this the will of God for you, or are you using your decision-making capacity to rebel, instead of doing what Jesus said?

> *Be angry, and yet do not sin; do not let the sun go down on your anger, and do not give the devil an opportunity [a place] (Eph 4:26, 27).*

2. What Is Repentance?

Central to forgiveness is the concept of repentance. In the Old Testament, the Hebrew word for repentance is *teschubah*, meaning to "return" (to God). Note that it lacks any implication of self-condemnation.

In the New Testament, the Greek word for repentance is *metaonia;* it means to "have another mind," to turn around and go the other way. It means something far more than feeling sorry; it means an abrupt change in direction.

Heart-based forgiveness takes place when we experience a change in our heart, an inner turning around. We let go of our desire to punish or get revenge and instead choose another direction—to release our debtor.

Mistakenly, we often confuse repentance and remorse. Remorse is a feeling of deep regret, of hopelessness, and even of despair. But remorse does not lead to constructive change, nor does it help us to turn toward God.

> *I now rejoice ... that you were made sorrowful to the point of repentance ... For the sorrow that is according to the will of God produces a repentance without regret, leading to salvation, but the sorrow of the world produces death (2 Cor 7:9-10).*

Reproof or condemnation?

Many Christians suffer from condemnation because of ignorance. They do not recognize the difference between reproof from the Lord and condemnation from the enemy.

According to Beall, [51] condemnation tears us down and discourages us, but God's reproof is uplifting and helpful. Condemnation brings vagueness, telling us we are wrong but not providing constructive feedback. Reproof from the

Holy Spirit comes as truth and light, making evident both the problem and the solution.

The Bible tells us that God never uses condemnation in dealing with us; we do not have to put up with condemning thoughts and feelings. When the Holy Spirit deals with us, even about forgiving someone, He does it according to the law of the Spirit of life in Christ Jesus (See Rom 8:1-2).

The law of sin and death (the Old Covenant, the Law of Moses) always brings condemnation to us, whereas the law of the Spirit of life in Christ Jesus (the New Covenant, the law of faith in Jesus Christ) always ministers life to us. We need to come to the place where we know the source of our feelings of condemnation and turn to our faith in Jesus Christ and his righteousness.

Repentance is for sinners

Until we come to the place where we recognize that we are sinners too—not just the person who hurt us—God cannot do very much for us. In his Sermon on the Mount, Jesus tries to help us understand this. He says "Blessed are the poor in spirit … those who mourn and weep … those who hunger and thirst for righteousness" (Matt 5:3-5).

> *It is not those who are healthy who need a physician, but those who are sick. But go and learn what this means, "I desire compassion, and not sacrifice," for I did not come to call the righteous, but sinners (Matt 9:13).*

We need to come to the end of ourselves and see our own poverty, that we are indeed sinners. Then it becomes easier to forgive those who failed us.

Biblical repentance occurs when we *turn away from sin* and *go toward God.* It opens us to receive the next gift of grace from God—faith.

3. What Is Faith?

In the New Testament, faith (*pistis*) means to be fully persuaded, convinced. Faith is far more than an idea, an emotion, or a mental belief; it means persuasion—confidence and assurance in the heart that what God says is true (Rom 4:20-21).

> *Faith is the assurance of things hoped for, the conviction [or substance or evidence] of things not seen (Heb 11:1).*
>
> *Being fully assured that what God had promised, He was able also to perform (Rom 4:21).*
>
> *The word is near you, in your mouth and in your heart—that is the word of faith which we are preaching, that if you confess with your mouth Jesus as Lord, and believe in your heart that God raised Him from the dead, you shall be saved (Rom 10:6-10).*

Faith essential in heart-based forgiveness

Repentance and faith towards God are two sides of the same coin. To experience the "resurrection effect" when we forgive, we must both repent and apply our faith in God. Faith opens the doorway to the presence of God. In repentance, we are *turning away from* something, and in faith, we are *turning towards* something.

> *Repent therefore and return, that your sins may be wiped away (Acts 3:19).*

It seems that forgiving others and answered prayer go together. Jesus says that we can receive what we pray for, as long as we believe. But he also says that, along with our praying, we must forgive anyone we have something against. Could this faith-forgiveness connection be because unforgiveness hinders our ability to believe God when we pray?

According to your faith be it unto you (Matt 9:29).

Have faith in God. Truly I say to you, whoever says to this mountain, 'be taken up and cast into the sea', and does not doubt in his heart, but believes that what he says is going to happen, it shall be granted him. Therefore I say to you, all things for which you pray and ask, believe that you have received then, and they shall be granted you (Mark 11:21-24).

Reflection

1. How has someone's sin (offense) affected your life?
2. What is the relationship between sin and hurt?
3. Why might unforgiveness prevent answered prayers?

10

Why Do We Not Forgive?

There were those who dwelt in darkness and in the shadow of death, prisoners in misery and chains, because they had rebelled against the words of God, and spurned the counsel of the Most High (Ps 107:10-11).

Recognizing the marvelous blessings that forgiveness brings, it's important to ask why so many of God's people refuse to do what Jesus said—forgive from their heart. Here are some ideas; perhaps you'll think of more.

Ignorance of Forgiveness

One reason for not forgiving is that we are ignorant of what it entails. Sometimes we are simply unaware that we need to forgive. The hurtful experience may have happened when we were very young, or we may have forgotten the sinful offense because it happened many years ago.

Hurt and unforgiveness dropped deep into our subconscious, and bitterness took root in our heart. Regions of the subconscious are below the level of our awareness, and we do not always know what lies within.

Other times we may have denied the unjust injury, believing it never happened. Or we may have deceived ourselves into thinking we have forgiven. We said the words "I forgive," but our heart never let go of the unjust offense. And the tangled roots of resentment, revenge, and hatred live on deep within us.

Hidden from sight, we are unaware that we are nurturing the offense in our heart. We are oblivious of how many times we recite our list of grievances or of the edge of bitterness on the words we speak. Others hear it, but we do not.

Rebellion Against God

Since the Garden of Eden, human beings have been in rebellion against God, resisting Him, his Word, and the Holy Spirit at every turn in the road. Because of our rebellious nature, we want to stay in control, believing we know what is best for us. Thus we do not want to do what Jesus said and forgive the people who hurt us.

Because we are kin to the Great Spirit, we want to seize the position of power and authority of the Father of all Spirits. We deceive ourselves about our motives and thus distort our view of the world and our place in it.

- We desire to be God, to take our own revenge.
- We harden our heart and ignore the "inner voice" of the Holy Spirit.

In trying to contend against our Creator, we try to live *over* the law and insist upon getting our own way. We think of ourselves as Little Orphan Annie or even a Superhero for God. We are blind and just don't recognize it.

We don't see ourselves living in rebellion against God. But his view is that we are not pitiably deprived innocents, but rather arrogant rebels who have misused their gifts.

We human beings search for every way possible to usurp the *position and power that God has*. That's because we don't know experientially and individually our own identity and purpose—let alone our union with the Father. So we feel lost, weak, and powerless, wandering around in inner darkness.

> *Therefore He humbled their heart with labor; they stumbled and there was none to help. Then they cried out to the Lord in their trouble; He saved them out of their distresses. He brought them out of darkness and the shadow of death, and broke their bands apart (Ps 107:12-14).*

> *Fools, because of their rebellious way, and because of their iniquities, were afflicted. Their soul abhorred all kinds of food; and they drew near to the gates of death. Then they cried out to the Lord in their trouble; He saved them out of their distresses. He sent His word and healed them, and delivered them from their destructions. (Ps 107:17-20).*

Ignorance of the Power of the Cross

Forgiveness is made possible because of the work of Jesus on the cross. All that Jesus did for us on the cross is factual, but we must have revelation of it in our hearts. God's truths must be seen and known in our heart as well as our mind, if we want to benefit from them. We must allow the Holy Spirit to bring us revelation of the power of the cross.

Here is a vivid account of one man's encounter with the reality of the cross:

> **A vision of the cross**
>
> I was standing out in the middle of a violent storm; it was dark and raining, with thunder and lightning all around me. I was amazed—but I couldn't figure out where I was. A moment before, I was in a church full of people worshipping God. Next moment I'm in the middle of this storm.
>
> Then the lightning flashed again, and off to my left, I could see a low hill with three crosses on top of it.

> **Suddenly the center cross was brightly illuminated, filled with light, with a radiance as brilliant as the sun. Spears of light were going up into the sky, down into the earth, and off to both sides. It felt like the light pierced right through me too.**
>
> **I cried out, "My God, it is all for real!" and the reality of Jesus Christ and the cross and Him crucified, entered into my heart and I began to weep. Growing up Catholic, I heard the story of Jesus and the cross, but now the reality entered my heart. It wasn't just a story anymore—it was a reality.**
>
> **I was somehow taken back to the terrible storm talked about in the Scriptures the night Jesus was crucified. It was real: I felt the rain and the wind; I saw the lighting and the cross. I will never forget it; whenever I think of it today, it is still as clear as the night it happened. (Ralph Nault)**

Pray for revelation of the cross

We made an audio recording of our friend relating his encounter with the cross. Later my husband replayed it and keyed it into a Word document. As he listened, the reality of the cross suddenly became alive to him too. The revelation came just by listening to our friend recount the vision—even though it had occurred some years earlier.

St. Paul recognizes the need for revelation when he prays for the saints at Ephesus:

> *That the God of our Lord Jesus Christ, the Father of glory, may give to you a spirit of wisdom and of revelation in the knowledge of Him. I pray that the eyes of your heart may be enlightened, so that you may know what is the hope of His calling (Eph 1:17-18).*

More Reasons Why We Don't Forgive

Some other reasons for not forgiving are because we:

1. Take all the blame, think it's our fault—what's wrong with me?—and not the unjust action of someone else.
2. Believe our role is to be a martyr, so we deliberately choose to suffer from the sins of others.
3. Think we are being good by denying or minimizing what happened.
4. Don't want to admit we were hurt.
5. Dread feeling the pain, because it hurts too much, so we can't possibly forgive.
6. Are numb, unable to feel our own feelings.
7. Want to make someone feel the pain we've felt or punish them.
8. Believe hanging on to anger empowers and protects us from being hurt again.
9. Enjoy being angry and plotting revenge.
10. Are afraid of condoning someone's unjust action.
11. Fear letting go of the hope of ever righting the wrong or getting retribution.
12. Think forgiveness is aimed at reconciliation, requiring us to continue a relationship with our offender.
13. Need deliverance from an evil spirit—a spirit of anger, revenge, etc.
14. Regard the blood of Jesus as not enough for our offender's sin, so we must make them pay for it.

Reflection

1. Can you explain why forgiveness must take place in the heart?
2. Why do you think people fail to forgive others?
3. How can the cross empower us to forgive?

11

Blessings of Forgiveness

> *Repent therefore and return, that your sins may be wiped away, in order that times of refreshing may come from the presence of the Lord (Acts 3:19).*

According to the Bible, we can chose between life and death, the blessing and the curse. Blessings come from God when we listen to Him and do what He says. Turning away from the Lord moves us out from under God's *protection*. We open ourselves to divine judgment and curses.

> *I have set before you life and death, the blessing and the curse. So choose life in order that you may live, you and your descendants, by loving the Lord your God, by obeying His voice (Deut 30:19-20).*

The intent of a curse is to release negative spiritual power against someone or something. The intent of a blessing is to release positive, godly, spiritual power on the person. Forgiveness opens the door to the kingdom of God and brings us divine blessings.[52]

Opens Us to God's Grace and Peace

As the Holy Spirit leads, we must make peace in our heart with everyone who has failed us in some way, including our self. When we forgive the people who have wronged us, we are doing what Jesus told us to do. In releasing others from our judgment, we are opening ourselves to God's grace and peace.

St. Paul understood the grace of God. His mission was "to testify solemnly of the gospel of the grace of God" (Acts 20:24). He wrote to the believers in Rome that "those who receive the abundance of grace and of the gift of righteousness will reign in life through the One, Jesus Christ" (Rom 5:17). Because of grace, we do not need to feel like victims in life.

The miracle of grace

The author of Hebrews warns us not to come short of God's *grace,* lest a root of bitterness grows in our hearts (Heb 12:15). In fact, we are encouraged to let our hearts be strengthened with *grace,* rather than with food (Heb 13:9).

According to Strong's Concordance, grace refers to divine influence acting upon the heart and manner of life. Thus, to "grow in grace" suggests that we increase our ability to rely on grace and our awareness of grace in our daily lives. The complete work of Jesus Christ has opened the doorway for us to enter into the throne room of God and receive his grace for everything we need (see 2 Cor 9:8; 12:9).

Psychiatrist M. Scott Peck[53] recognized the existence of "a powerful force originating outside of human consciousness which nurtures the spiritual growth" of his clients. He found grace to be a very common phenomenon that cannot be explained within the conceptual framework of conventional science and natural law.

Although grace is an extraordinary power extended to us, too often we resist it.

Stuck in my anger

Many years ago I had an experience with God's grace that left its mark in me. At the time I was very angry with my husband (for what, I no longer remember); actually I was stuck in my anger, not able to let go of it.

Suddenly I felt my anger begin to dissipate, but I resisted letting it go—I wanted to stay angry. In that moment, the Lord spoke to me: *"If you resist my grace now, you will not receive it again."* This got my attention! I knew it was the Lord.

Immediately I became willing to let go of the anger and allow God's grace to flow into my heart again. I did not allow my heart to become hard! I knew that grace from God was something to be highly valued, even though I didn't understand it yet.

Since then I have experienced God's grace numerous times. Slowly I have learned to treasure grace and to rely upon it. When I am stuck in some life-negating attitude, I more quickly cry out, "Lord, I am helpless to get out of this; please send me your grace. I will wait until you send it. Thank You."

Keeps us from hurting those we love

Eating something bitter leaves a biting, disagreeable sensation in the mouth. Similarly bitterness in the heart causes life to taste bitter. We find little joy in living life and we infect others with our bitterness.

When we do not go to God and receive his grace for the pain inflicted by others, unforgiveness turns inward, becomes deep-seated, and bitterness gets rooted in our hearts. We are warned of this consequence in the Bible:

> *See to it that no one comes short of the grace of God; that no root of bitterness springing up causes trouble, and by it many have been defiled (Heb 12:15).*

According to the Bible, bitterness rooted in the heart affects the very words we speak: "For the mouth speaks out of that which fills the heart" (Matt 12:34). People with a root of bitterness have a tonal quality that sounds sharp, edgy, sarcastic—perhaps reproachful or even cruel.

Interestingly, reproach can break the heart of a child (Ps 69:20). Words spoken in a critical tone can penetrate to the psychological center of the child. However, if the parent's voice is kind, gentle, and peaceful, the child's inner core will be filled with the knowledge that she/he is safe and loved.

Empowers us to be free from destructive relationships

Forgiveness enables us to receive God's grace and empowers us to break free from ungodly relationships or soul ties.[54] Ungodly soul ties are created when a person seeks to dominate, manipulate, or control another—perhaps through violence, fear, or abuse.

These destructive relationships create avenues for sinful energies to be released and trouble the person who is being dominated, manipulated, or controlled.[55] Forgiveness is the powerful key that frees you and enables God's healing presence to flow.

Frees Our Conscience from Guilt

Guilt damages our capacity to love others and to love ourselves. It manipulates us, influencing our choices and the motivations in our heart. It closes us off from intimate relationships with the people around us.

According to Mowrer, "The thing that most seriously damages our capacity to love and to be lovable is not neglect or rejection by others, but unacknowledged and un-atoned personal guilt—whether true or false."[56]

Forgiving people who unjustly wrong us enables us to find freedom from our failures, mistakes, and transgressions. Jesus said we will be forgiven if we forgive those people who sinned against us.

> *For if you forgive others for their transgressions, Your heavenly Father will also forgive you: But if you do not forgive others, then your Father will not forgive your transgressions (Matt 6:14-15).*

I cannot forgive me

My husband had a problem forgiving himself about how he'd failed our son who needed help with fixing his mini-bike:

"Compulsively working in my garden, I didn't respond to his need for help. Through the years I often thought, *I will never forgive myself for this.*

As Judith and I talked about this, I realized that my unwillingness to forgive myself was negatively impacting my relationship with my son. Whenever I'd try to relate to him, I'd look at him through my eyes of guilt. Thus the flow of love from my own heart was impeded. When I finally did the hard work of forgiving myself, my tormenting guilt subsided."

Destructive power of false guilt

We were praying with a woman in Germany about a trauma involving the death of her father in WWII. Incredibly, the father of lies had told her she was responsible for her father's death—even though she'd been only two years old when he died! This false guilt had affected her entire life. As the Lord brought his healing truths into her memory, she cried out, "I don't have to be manipulated by guilt any longer!"

Enables Our Prayers to Be Answered

Forgiving others is a necessary condition to answered prayers, especially when we are praying for healing in our bodies. Jesus tells us we can receive the things we pray for—if we believe. Then he says, whenever we stand praying, we are to forgive anyone we have something against.

Why does Jesus connect faith and forgiveness? Is it because unforgiveness in our heart makes it impossible to believe that God will answer our prayers?

> *I say to you, all things for which you pray and ask, believe that you have received them, and they shall be granted you. And whenever you stand praying, forgive, if you have anything against any; that your Father also which is in heaven may forgive you your trespasses (Mark 11:24-25).*

Frees Us from the Enemy

We are the ones who benefit the most by choosing to forgive others. Forgiving our debtor frees us from the power of the enemy in that area of our lives. Until the offenders assume responsibility for their unjust behavior and repent, they stay the same. But we change—we gain more freedom.

Releases us from the past

Our feelings of resentment, anger, and desire for revenge are destructive emotions that do us great harm, actually holding us in bondage to the past. These feelings will continue to rob us of our God-given creative energy for living. Like Lot's wife, we are not free to move forward into the future and live full, satisfying lives.

True heart-based forgiveness releases us from the people who have wounded us and are keeping us bound to our painful past. Forgiving enables us to continue to grow in our ability to embrace life and love in the present.

Frees us from painful memories

It is vital that we forgive everyone who has ever hurt us or failed us in some way and forgive ourselves for our own failures and mistakes—if we want our wounds to be healed. The inability to forgive others is a crucial barrier to experiencing the healing presence of Jesus Christ in our wounds.

> **Forgiving my father leads to healing**
>
> When my husband forgave his father, it opened the doorway for deep inner healing reaching back many years. Here is his story:
>
> "Reflecting on my youth, I feel that my father did not see me or hear me; he seemed not to recognize my existence, accept me, and affirm my life. As an adult I blamed my father for my own failures in life.
>
> One day I was finally able to reach a deep level of true forgiveness. Acutely aware of my own abject failure as a husband, and badly in need of forgiveness for myself, how could I not forgive someone else? In an appointment with God, two men led me through the *Freedom in Christ* procedure.[57]
>
> As part of the forgiveness step, I forgave my father and surrendered my judgment of him. I withdrew all my *expectations* of my father and released him from my demands upon him. Forgiving my father opened up many other areas for inner healing in my life."

Refreshes Us Through God's Presence

We experience great loss when we do not understand the importance of forgiveness and how it influences our relationship with God. According to the Scriptures, unforgiveness blocks our ability to see God and know his abiding presence within us.

> *If we love one another, God abides in us, and His love is perfected in us (1 John 4:12).*

Chronic anger, hostility, and hatred clog up and cut off the flow of God's life within us. The roar of emotions easily overpowers the small, delicate motions of the spirit, and gradually the accumulation of negative emotions cuts off our sensitivity to the voice of the Spirit of God.

> *Walk no longer just as the Gentiles also walk ... excluded from the life of God, because of the ignorance that is in them, because of the hardness of their heart (Eph 4:17-18).*

When you repent and forgive from your heart the people who hurt you, then you will be refreshed by the presence of the Lord in your spirit.

Reflection

1. Which of the above blessings do you feel the need for?
2. Listen to the people around you and notice if you recognize a root of bitterness.
3. Why is guilt so destructive?

12

It's Time to Forgive

Let all bitterness and wrath [rage] and anger and clamor [brawling] and slander, be put away from you along with all malice. And be kind to one another, tender-hearted, forgiving each other, just as God in Christ also has forgiven you (Eph 4:31-32).

Now we're ready to utilize the great tool of power God has given to humanity: forgiveness. Because of the sacrificial blood of Jesus Christ on the cross, you can make peace in your heart with everyone who has ever hurt you.

Get that cleared up before God. Forgive your father and mother, and all other family or friends, for what they did or did not do for you. Your heart needs to be cleansed from all bitter judgments, resentments, anger, hate, and murder, so you can experience God's peace, joy, and healing in your life.

And don't forget: you might need to forgive yourself. You cannot come to a place of peace as long as you are holding judgments against yourself. No one is benefiting from your refusal to accept the blood of Jesus as enough for your failures; to the contrary, you are hurting your family and friends.

Preparing to Forgive

Note: Before you begin this process, I suggest you review Chapter 8, *Pathway to Heart-Based Forgiveness.* That discussion describes in detail how to let go of an offense at a deep heart level. Acknowledging your wounding and taking an account of what happened helps to prepare you to release the offender from the debt they owe you.

1. Ask the Lord to search your heart

Ask the Lord to show you any resentment, anger, vengeful feelings, or bitterness in your mind and heart. Because resentments and bitterness are often concealed in painful memories, we can ask the Lord if there is any pain in us, like the Psalmist did:

> *Search me O God, and know my heart; Try me and know my anxious thoughts; and see if there be any way of pain in me (Ps 139:23-24).*

As you pray, God may bring to mind people and experiences you have totally forgotten. Let Him do it, even if it is painful. Remember, you are doing this for your sake, not the ones who hurt you.

Do not rationalize or explain the person's behavior. Forgiveness is you dealing with your pain and leaving the other person to God. Positive feelings will follow in time; freeing yourself from the past is the critical issue right now.

2. Start a list of the people you are holding a debt against

Consider people in your family of origin

Think of the people in your family—even those who are no longer alive—and ask yourself if anyone owes you something: your father, mother, sister, brother, grandmother, grandfather, aunts, uncles, etc. What did they do to you or not do for you?

Dear Heavenly Father, I thank you that I belong to you. I want to honor my mother and my father, but I also know that my family is not perfect. I ask you to reveal to me who I need to forgive.

Watch to see whose face makes you uncomfortable, who you do not like, who you disapprove of. Pay attention to what you feel in the pit of your stomach. Does your stomach tighten? Or is there a reaction inside when you think of that person?

Then write their name down, like this:

I need to forgive my ____________________ *(write down their name).*

Consider other people

Look around you and ask who makes you feel uncomfortable, who you do not like, who you disapprove of: husband, wife, son, daughter, daughter-in-law, son-in-law, mother-in-law, father-in-law, teacher, pastor, neighbor, employer, co-worker, boy/girlfriend, former partner, etc.

As you think of them—even if they are no longer alive—pay attention to what you feel in the pit of your stomach. Does your stomach tighten? Or is there a "high octane ping in your spirit" when you think of that person?[58] Add their name to your list:

I need to forgive ______________________________ *(write down their name).*

At the end of your list write "myself"

Forgiving yourself is accepting God's cleansing and forgiveness for your failures. It is amazingly difficult for people to forgive themselves. It seems we are more ready to forgive others rather than our self. One woman said to me, "God has to forgive me; that's his job, but I don't have to forgive me."

I need to forgive myself ______________________________ _______ (write down your name).

Do you need to forgive God?

Thoughts raised up against the knowledge of God will usually result in angry feelings toward Him. Technically, we can't forgive God because He cannot commit any sin. But we need to specifically renounce any way that we hold God or Jesus or the Holy Spirit responsible for events in our life. We must agree to release any anger we have toward them.

I need to forgive ____________________ (write down who in the deity you need to forgive).

3. Next, write out exactly why you need to forgive each person:

What was the wrong thing they did to you or failed to do for you? How did they sin against you?

Write out the specific way they hurt you.

I need to forgive (name) for _________________ (describe what their sin was).

State what their sin cost you or what it is you want from them

Identify exactly what you think their debt is. What do they owe you? What do you expect from them? Describe how their sin has impacted your life. What has it cost you?

He or she owes me ______________________(write it out).

4. Identify how their sin made you feel

Acknowledge what you felt. Admit to yourself, what he/she did made me feel … . True heart-based forgiveness must go deep, touching our emotional core.

Because it made me feel____________________ (put a name on the feeling).

5. Release your feelings to God

You may find it helpful to write a letter to God about what happened. Start with "Dear Heavenly Father," then write down everything that comes to mind, without judging or censoring it. Don't think about what you are writing; just write spontaneously, allowing the words to quickly flow.

This will help you get in touch with your emotions and release your feelings to God. Remember to sign your name when you are finished.

Doing Business with God

(The following ideas have been drawn from Ed Smith, Charles Zeiders, Mark & Patti Virkler, Derek Prince, Neil Anderson, and Agnes Sanford.)

1. Welcome the Holy Spirit's presence to guide and empower you

Position your heart in humility before the Lord. Give your heart to God now. Confess aloud your faith in Jesus Christ and his sacrifice on your behalf. Acknowledge that it is solely on the basis of what Jesus has done on your behalf that you can be forgiven, forgive others, and forgive yourself. Declare your total dependence on God to free you.

Heavenly Father, I need you to make me clean and whole. I am coming to you to confess my unforgiveness as sin and allow you to cleanse me of all unrighteousness. I ask you for your complete forgiveness. I believe that the Lord Jesus Christ is the Son of God and the only way to God, and that He died on the cross for my sins and rose again from the dead. I give up all my rebellion and all my sins, and I submit myself to you as my Lord.

2. Forgive each person on your list, praying aloud

Make a decision to forgive all the people who have ever hurt you, recognizing that holding bitterness produces death in you and in those around you.

Speak out loud the words of forgiveness. You will verbalize your decision by saying out loud, "Lord, I forgive … ." Name the person or persons involved and state specifically what their sin is and how it made you feel.

Lord, I choose to forgive (name) for (state specifically what their sin was), because it made me feel (state your feelings).

Don't say, "Lord, please help me to forgive," because He is already helping you. Do not say, "Lord, I want to forgive," because you are bypassing the hard-core choice to forgive, which is your responsibility.

Here is an example of how you can do this:

Lord Jesus, I choose not to hold on to my bitterness and anger. I choose to forgive (name) for (what they did), because it made me feel (verbally share with the Lord every hurt and how it made you feel).

I renounce all my sins involved in holding unforgiveness against (name) and I choose not to hold on to my resentment. I give up my right to be angry with (name). I relinquish my right to seek revenge. I release (name) into your hands.

Make me clean and whole and release me from this sin. I thank you that your blood is enough for every sin committed against me. I thank you for the power of your blood to cleanse my heart from all resentment, bitterness, anger, rage, etc. I now receive your forgiveness.

Thank you for setting me free from the bondage of my bitterness. I now ask you to bless those who have hurt me. In Jesus' name, I pray. Amen.

3. Ask the Lord to heal your wounds

You may need to be healed of the consequences of sins. After you have forgiven every person for every painful memory, then finish this step by praying:

Lord, I release all these people to you, into your hands, and I ask you to reveal the negative beliefs that were the result of their sins and to heal my damaged emotions and painful wounds. In Jesus' name I pray. Amen.

Once you forgive your debtor, your desire for retaliation dissipates and your wounds can be comforted by the healing grace of God. We will know we have truly released someone from their trespass against us when we think of it and feel only a rush of joy and love; then we have forgiveness (Unknown).

Reflection

1. Pay attention to the movements in your heart as you walk the pathway of forgiveness.
2. Did you experience a subtle change in your heart? A moment of compassion?
3. After you have forgiven, watch for some sense of "the resurrection effect" (see Chapter 1).

Blessing

To you who are doing the hard work of heart-based forgiveness, I offer you the reassuring words spoken by the prophet Isaiah: I speak comfort to you, I call out to you that your warfare has ended, that your iniquity has been removed (see Isa 40:1-2).

Judith A. Doctor

References

Anderson, Neil T. *The Steps To Freedom in Christ.* Grand Rapids, MI: Bethany House, 2004.

Aponte, Harry J. "Love, the spiritual wellspring of forgiveness: an example of spirituality in therapy." *Journal of Family Therapy* 20 (1998): 37--58.

Banks, Bill & Sue. *Breaking Unhealthy Soul-Ties.* Kirkwood, MO: Impact Christian Books, 1999.

Beall, James Lee. *Laying The Foundation.* South Plainfield, NJ: Bridge Publishing, 1976.

Caine, W. & Kaufman, B. Prayer, *Faith, and Healing.* Emmaus, PA: Rodale Press, 1999.

Dayton, Tian, Ph.D. *The Living Stage.* Deerfield Beach, FL: Health Communications, 2005.

DiBlasio, F. "The role of social workers' beliefs in helping family members forgive." *Families in Society* 74(3), 1993.

Enright, Robert. "Forgiveness: Pathway to Healing." NACSW Podcast, October 18, 2013, http://www.nacsw.org/RC/49997374.mp3.

Enright, Robert. *The Forgiving Life.* Washington, D.C.: APA Books, 2012.

Freedman, S.R., & Enright, R.D. "Forgiveness is an intervention goal with incest survivors." *Journal of Consulting and Clinical Psychology* 64 (1996): 982-983.

Fromm, Erich. *The Heart of Man.* New York, NY: Harper & Row, 1964.

Hodge, D. "Spiritual assessment: A review of major qualitative methods and a new framework for assessing spirituality." *Social Work* 46(3) (2001).

International Forgiveness Institute. http://internationalforgiveness.com/why-forgive.htm.

Kylstra, Chester & Betsy. *Restoring the Foundations: An Integrated Approach To Healing Ministry*, 2nd Ed. Hendersonville, NC: Proclaiming His Word Publications, 1994.

Linn, Matt & Dennis & Fabricant, Sheila. *Healing the Eight Stages of Life.* New York: Paulist Press, 1988.

Long, Brad & Strickler, Cindy. *Let Jesus Heal Your Hidden Wounds: Cooperating With The Holy Spirit in Healing Ministry.* Grand Rapids, MI: Chosen Books, 2001.

McKay, Matt, & Paleg, Kim. *Focal Group Psychotherapy.* Oakland, CA: New Harbinger Publications, Inc., 1992.

Mowrer, O. Hobart. *The New Group Therapy.* Princeton, NJ: D. Van Nostrand Company, 1964.

Nault, Ralph, *There Is More: Discovering New Depths Of Spiritual Understanding.* 2014. (www.ralphnault.com)

Peale, Norman Vincent. *The Power of Positive Thinking.* New York: Prentice-Hall, Inc., 1952.

Peck, M. Scott. *The Road Less Traveled.* New York: Simon and Schuster, 1980.

Prince, Derek. *Blessing or Curse: You Can Choose.* Grand Rapids, MI: Chosen Books, 1990.

Sandford, John & Paula. *The Transformation of the Inner Man.* So. Plainfield, NJ: Bridge Publishing, Inc., 1982.

Sanford, Agnes. *The Healing Light.* New York: Ballantine Books, 1947/1992.

Smith, Ed. *Beyond Tolerable Recovery.* Campbellsville, KY: Family Care Publishing, 1999.

Virkler, Mark & Patti. *Prayers That Heal the Heart.* Gainesville, FL: Bridge-Logos, 2001.

Weinberg, N. "Does apologizing help? The role of self-blame and making amends in recovery from bereavement." *Health & Social Work* 20(4), (1995): 294-299.

Wright, Henry, W. *A More Excellent Way: Spiritual Roots of Disease; Pathways to Wholeness.* Thomaston, GA: Pleasant Valley Publications, 2005.

Zeiders, Charles, L, Ph.D. "A Christian Depth Psychology of Forgiveness Leading To The Resurrection Effect." *The Journal of Christian Healing* 21, no. 2 (Summer, 1999).

About Judith A. Doctor

Author, speaker, mentor, Judith A. Doctor (MSW, RN) conducts groups, retreats, and individual sessions for spiritual growth and healing. Co-founder of Kairos Ministries, Inc., Judith integrates her professional knowledge with her spiritual gifts, calling, and anointing to facilitate redemptive and restorative moments through the Holy Spirit.

Her life is marked by numerous transformative encounters with the living God. She knows firsthand a loving God who brought resurrection life through the crises of her life—death of a child from leukemia, battle-worn marriage, family addictions, and deep inside her troubled soul. Changed by the grace of God, she carries a confident authority to help others become all that God intended for them.

A spiritual adventurer, Judith has responded to the call of God to go into the highways and byways of life. Her stories of the transformative power of God and how she was led by the Holy Spirit have inspired and strengthened many in the USA and Europe. Speaking from her heart, she connects with her audience at a deep level, enabling them to open their hearts and receive something more from the Lord.

Since 1980, Judith has addressed such diverse groups as parish nurses, social workers, Romanian Nurses, German clinics, Protestant and Catholic churches, and recovery groups. Her ministry includes a monthly radio program on Christian spirituality broadcast live from Germany.

Judith coauthored two books on dreams from a Judeo-Christian perspective. In addition, she has published in the

Journal of Christian Healing, and in *Asociația De Nursing Din România Journal.*

Her hobbies include chats with friends, evening bike rides, studying, spiritual-political discourse, art exhibits, and morning coffee with her husband, Gerald. Married for more than fifty-seven years, they have two sons and daughters-in-law, and four grandchildren.

Contact Judith via email: judith@judithdoctor.com

Notes

Chapter 1 When You Stand Praying, Forgive

1 David Hodge, "Spiritual assessment: A review of major qualitative methods and a new framework for assessing spirituality," *Social Work* 46(3), (2001).

2 Charles Zeiders, "A Christian Depth Psychology of Forgiveness Leading To The Resurrection Effect," *The Journal of Christian Healing* 21, no. 2 (Summer, 1999).

3 Tian Dayton, *The Living Stage* (Deerfield Beach, FL: Health Communications, Inc., 2005), 492.

4 O. Hobart Mowrer, *The New Group Therapy* (Princeton, NJ: D. Van Nostrand Company, 1964), 27.

5 As cited in Mark Butler, Samuel Dahlin, & Stephen Fife, "Languaging Factors Affecting Clients' Acceptance Of Forgiveness Intervention In Marital Therapy," *Journal of Marital & Family Therapy* 28(3) (July 2002): 285-298. http://faculty.unlv.edu/fifes2/pdf/Languaging%20of%20Forgiveness.pdf

6 F. DiBlasio, "The role of social workers' beliefs in helping family members forgive," *Families in Society* 74(3), 163-170.

7 D.L. Fennel, (1993), as cited in Mark Butler, Samuel Dahlin, & Stephen Fife, "Languaging Factors Affecting Clients' Acceptance Of Forgiveness Intervention In Marital Therapy," *Journal of Marital & Family Therapy* 28(3) (July 2002): 285-298. (http://faculty.unlv.edu/fifes2/pdf/Languaging%20of%20Forgiveness.pdf)

8 Harry J. Aponte, "Love, the spiritual wellspring of forgiveness: An example of spirituality in our therapy," *Journal of Family Therapy* (U. K) (20(1) (February, 1998): 39.

9 Zeiders, "A Christian Depth Psychology of Forgiveness."

10 Agnes Sanford, *The Healing Gifts of the Spirit* (San Francisco, CA: Harper & Row, 1996), 100.

11 Zeiders, "A Christian Depth Psychology of Forgiveness," 32.

Chapter 2 High Cost of Unforgiveness

12 Norman Vincent Peale, *The Power of Positive Thinking* (New York: Prentice-Hall, Inc., 1952), 188.

13 Matt McKay & Kim Paleg, *Focal Group Psychotherapy* (Oakland, CA: New Harbinger Publications, Inc., 1992)
14 Francis MacNutt. *Healing* (Notre Dame, IN: Ava Maria Press, 1974), 153.
15 McKay & Paleg, *Focal Group Psychotherapy.*
16 Henry W. Wright, *A More Excellent Way: Spiritual Roots of Disease; Pathways to Wholeness* (Thomaston, GA: Pleasant Valley Publications, 2005).
17 MacNutt, *Healing,* 155.
18 Peale, *The Power of Positive Thinking,* 189-197.
19 Bill & Sue Banks, *Breaking Unhealthy Soul-Ties* (Kirkwood, MO: Impact Christian Books, 1999).

Chapter 3 Downward Spiral of Unforgiveness

20 McKay & Paleg, *Focal Group Psychotherapy.*
21 McKay & Paleg, *Focal Group Psychotherapy.*
22 Dan B. Allender & Tremper Longman, *Cry Of The Soul, How Our Emotions Reveal Our Deepest questions About God* (Colorado Springs, CO: NavPress, 1994), 46.
23 McKay & Paleg, *Focal Group Psychotherapy.*
24 Ibid.

Chapter 4 Balancing the Scales of Justice

25 Agnes Sanford, *The Healing Light* (New York, NY: Ballantine Books, 1947/1992), 5.
26 Paul Billheimer, *Destined To Overcome: The Technique Of Spiritual Warfare (*Minneapolis, MN: Bethany House Publishers, 1982).
27 John & Paula Sandford, *The Transformation Of The Inner Man* (Tulsa, OK: Victory House, 1982), 239.
28 Ibid.
29 Ibid., 88.
30 Sin means to miss the mark or the road.

Chapter 5 Forgiveness Requires Blood

31 Boris Matthews, Ed., *The Herder Symbol Dictionary of Symbols: Symbols from Art, Archeology, Mythology, Literature, and Religion* (New York: Continuum International Publishing Group, 1993) [Initially published as: Herder Lexikon & Boris Matthews, *The Herder Symbol Dictionary* (Brooklyn, NY: Chiron Publications, 1986)], 24.

Chapter 6 What Is Forgiveness?

32 *Sin* means to "miss the mark." (See Chapter 9)

33 Ed Smith, *Beyond Tolerable Recovery* (Campbellsville, KY: Family Care Publishing, 1999), 239.

34 Harry J. Aponte, "Love, the spiritual wellspring of forgiveness: an example of spirituality in therapy," *Journal of Family Therapy* 20 (1998): 37-58.

35 S.R. Freedman, R.D. Enright & Rique (1998, p. 47), as cited in R.S. Balkin, S.J. Freeman, & S.R. Lyman, "Forgiveness, reconciliation, and Mechila: integrating the Jewish concept of forgiveness into clinical practice," *American Counseling Association,* (Jan 2009) (http://www.highbeam.com/doc/1G1-191475601.html).

36 Zeiders, "A Christian Depth Psychology of Forgiveness," 32.

37 Robert Enright, *The Forgiving Life* (Washington, D.C.: APA Books, 2012).

38 W. Caine, & B. Kaufman, *Prayer, Faith, and Healing* (Emmaus, PA: Rodale Press, 1999).

39 Ed Smith, *Beyond Tolerable Recovery.*

40 Neil Anderson, *The Steps To Freedom in Christ* (Grand Rapids, MI: Bethany House, 2004).

41 Tian Dayton, *The Living Stage* (Deerfield Beach, FL: Health Communications, 2005).

42 Neil Anderson, *The Steps To Freedom in Christ.*

43 Tian Dayton, *The Living Stage*, 337.

Chapter 7 Misconceptions About Forgiveness

44 Ideas in this chapter have been adapted from Charles Zeiders, Caine & Kaufman, Ed Smith, Neil Anderson, and John & Paula Sandford.

45 Zeiders, "A Christian Depth Psychology of Forgiveness," 33.

Chapter 8 Pathway to Heart-Based Forgiveness

46 Ibid.

47 Ed Smith, *Beyond Tolerable Recovery.*

48 As cited by Charnicia E. Huggins, "Receiving an Apology Does a Body Good, Study Finds," *Reuters Health* (Oct 10, 2002). (http://www.rubysemporium.org/receiving_apology.html)

49 Zeiders, "A Christian Depth Psychology of Forgiveness," 33.

50 Ibid.

Chapter 9 Bedrock Truths of Christianity

51 James Beall, *Laying The Foundation* (South Plainfield, NJ: Bridge Publishing, 1976), 28.

Chapter 11 Blessings of Forgiveness

52 Derek Prince, *Blessing or Curse: You Can Choose* (Grand Rapids, MI: Chosen Books, 1990), 32.
53 Scott Peck, *The Road Less Traveled* (NY: Simon and Schuster, 1978).
54 Bill & Sue Banks, *Breaking Unhealthy Soul-Ties.*
55 Mark & Patti Virkler, *Prayers That Heal the Heart* (Gainesville, FL: Bridge-Logos, 2001), 31.
56 O. Hobart Mowrer, *The New Group Therapy*, 27.
57 Neil Anderson, *The Steps to Freedom in Christ.*

Chapter 12 It's Time to Forgive

58 Smith, *Beyond Tolerable Recovery.*

Dream Books by Judith A. Doctor

Today, more than ever, we need to hear what God is saying to us, and dreams are one way that He makes his word known to us. Dreams help us on every level of our lives—spiritual growth, personal wholeness, work, ministry, and our relationships with God, others, and ourselves.

Her books will help you understand dreams from a Christian perspective:

Christian Dreamwork: 33 Ways To Discover Divine Treasure In Dreams

A practical handbook that describes different ways to understand your dreams, it empowers you to relate to your own dreams and draw out their inner meaning.

The book explains the fundamental skills, strategies and techniques of Christian dreamwork so you can benefit from God's wise counsel in your dreams. As a spiritual practice, dreamwork can take on a sacredness, facilitating a closer relationship with God.

Dream Treasure: Learning the Language of Heaven

A well-researched—but easily approachable—comprehensive book on dreams from a Christian perspective. It provides a framework for 21st century believers to safely embrace dreams.

The book provides an understanding of the imaginative, pictorial language of symbolism to help you appreciate the messages in your dreams. Scriptural principles help you navigate the world of dreaming, including how to test the validity of a dream interpretation.

Purchase these helpful books on dreams from Amazon or any of the other major book sellers.